Kent Er Travel Guide , England.

The History, Towns and Cities

Author
Jacob Martinez

Publisher:
INFORMATION-SOURCE
16192 Coastal Highway
Lewes, DE 19958.

TABLE OF CONTENT

Summary

Kent County England: When you hear or see about traveling plan or engagement. Whether it be a great distance or just an hour away, travel is so important for your own character development. Not to mention that you get to experience new things with every place you have never been before. Traveling is the best way to get out of your comfort zone and invites you to experience life in different ways.

Traveling is something really unique, and there are only so many things we can learn in a school environment. Travel really can't be taught; you can learn about other cultures, but you can't be fully taught unless you experience it. Scientifically, it is shown that traveling also gains you more confidence and a great way to develop cultural sensitivity. Not to mention if you travel abroad, you can most likely be submerged into a second or third language.

To me, traveling is something that absolutely blows my mind. Seeing something that you have never seen before, being places that people live everyday and forget the beauty of their home and become absolutely in awe of the surroundings, and knowing that sometimes places are so different from where you're familiar.

I actually had the pleasure of visiting Syros, Greece for about a month, and let me tell you; that was the moment I knew I wanted to see the world. It was such an experience being with friends and seeing all these new things that I knew I may never get to see again. It's so important to take in every moment in when you're traveling. Even if it is a location easily accessible to you, because in the moment, you may never see that same thing again.

I cannot stress enough, if you have the financial ability to travel... pack up today. There is no way that if I had a large amount of money, that I would stay in one place for more than a day. There may be a lot of crazy things going on in the world at all times, but there's one thing that redeems all the bad; beauty.

About Kent, England

Introduction

It seems every travel guide is required to mention that Kent is known as "The Garden of England". There, consider it mentioned. For all that the phrase is overused and time-worn, there is truth to the saying. Kent is a county of delightful gardens, farmland, and orchards, attractive despite its proximity to London and the bustle of traffic heading south to the Channel ferry ports.

There are indeed so many outstanding gardens in Kent that it is difficult to know where to begin. How about Sissinghurst Castle, the wonderful creation of popular garden writer Vita Sackville-West? Sissinghurst was planted as a series of separate gardens within the larger garden around a Tudor tower house.

Or what about Beech Court, where the woodland garden surrounds a medieval farmhouse? At romantic Scotney

Castle the superb picturesque gardens tumble down the hillside to the ruins of a 14th-century moated manor, while the informal Emmet's Gardens at Idle Hill give wonderful views across the Weald of Kent.

There is, of course, more to Kent than gardens. The county is home to more country houses and buildings of historic interest per square mile than just about any place else in England, from the informal, like Smallhythe, where actress Ellen Terry occupied a delightful half-timbered Tudor cottage, to the grandiose, like Leeds Castle, which seems to float like a romantic lily-pad upon its lake.

Penshurst Place near Tonbridge is perhaps the finest late-medieval stately home in the country. Within Penshurst is the superb 14th century Baron's Hall, boasting a wooden beamed roof which soars fully 60 feet above the hall floor. Squerryes Court is a Jacobean manor in 10 acres of beautiful formal gardens, while Knole is an opulent treasure house, little altered since the 18th century when the Sackville family filled it with fine art and furniture.

Hever Castle was the childhood home of Anne Boleyn, and the moated manor is surrounded by beautiful Italianate gardens and a popular hedge maze. Chartwell, at Westerham, was the home of Winston Churchill, and the house has been left as it was during the great statesman's lifetime.

Chiddingstone Castle is a romantic vision in the picturesque style, yet it is a true castle, with roots going back to the Tudor era. It is just as well to stop this listing of historic houses here, and mention a few of the other delights of Kent - but there are scores more examples of wonderfully enjoyable houses to visit.

One of the most popular destinations in Kent is Dover; while the town itself suffers from urban growth, the grim Norman castle holds much historical interest. It was begun by Henry II as part of England's ongoing attempts to discourage French invasions. Beneath the castle is a maze of tunnels constructed to house Allied headquarters during WWII. A series of special exhibits and living history displays help bring that dark time to life.

Take the North Downs Way long-distance path inland from Dover and you come at last to Canterbury, the magnet that has drawn pilgrims to it for over 800 years. Canterbury Cathedral, scene of the martyrdom of Thomas a Becket, is the prime attraction, but the city itself is an attractive mix of new and old.

The first church here was founded by St. Augustine in 597, but the present building is primarily the product of the 12th century, with notable later additions. The precise spot where Becket was killed by four knights of Henry II is known, and cathedral guides recount the tale with suitable gusto to visitors.

Kent has something for everyone, from beautiful countryside and attractive villages, to grand houses and castles. Then, there are all those gardens.

The History

A brief history.

The name Kent derives from the ancient Celtic tribe who inhabited South East England from the Thames to the south coast. Their lands included modern Kent plus parts of Surrey, Sussex and Greater London. The Roman's called the people the Cantii or Cantiaci and the county Cantium. Julius Caesar wrote in his account of his military campaigns in northern Europe, *Gallic Wars*, that the people of Cantium were the most civilized of the Celtic tribes.

Julius Caesar visited Britain twice. The first occasion in 55 BC he landed at Deal and his fleet was defeated by the high tidal range which swamped their ships. In 54 BC Caesar returned with cavalry and won a significant skirmish at Canterbury; reputedly near to Bigbury Iron Age hill fort. After a short campaign in England Julius Caesar left our shores. In 43AD under Emperor Claudius the Roman's returned and stayed for almost four centuries.

The Ancient Britons did not have a written history so we have little knowledge of what they may have called Canterbury. Although it may have been a version of *Durovernum*, the name the Roman's used. This has linguistic roots to the Iron-Age tribes who lived on the British Isles before the Roman invasion. *Duro* roughly translates to fortified enclosure; vernum to marshy crossing with Alders. The first documentation of a name for Canterbury was in a 2nd century geography the *Antoine Itinerary*. In that the Roman named it *Durovernum Cantiacorum*. *Cantiacorum* meaning that the city was a Civitas Capital, that is a town where tribal leaders were trusted to rule their own people with the addition of Roman advisors. Canterbury was the principle tribal capital of Cantium (Kent) with a second area of administration at Rochester which the Roman's named: *Durobrivae Cantiacorum*. *Durobrivae* meaning fortified crossing with a bridge.

Man or Maid of Kent v Kentish Man or Maid

Kent's largest river is the Medway which divides the county vaguely east and west. Its source is in the High Weald Sussex. Its mouth flows in to the Thames estuary. Hasted wrote in his encyclopaedic work *The Historical & Topographical Survey of Kent* that the ancient Britons called the Medway *Vaga* (travel) to which the Saxons prefixed *Med* (middle). If you are born on the east side of the Medway you may call yourself a Man of Kent. If you were born to the west a Kentish Man. The female equivalent being Maids of Kent or Kentish Maids. When the Men and Maids terms first came in to use is uncertain. Some say its from the invasion of Angles, Saxons and Jutes who called Canterbury *Cantawarburgh*. The Anglo Saxons occupied West Kent whilst the Jutes, settled East of the Medway.

Others, as in this ode *Men of Kent & Kentish Men*[*], suggest that it dates from the Norman invasion when the Men of Kent refused to let the Conqueror pass through East Kent unless they were allowed to keep certain rights and privileges. This tale may have some truth behind it in that Kent was the only English county to keep the inheritance laws of Gavelkind after the conquest.

Norman and later

After the Battle of Hastings the Normans started a program of building works with castles and cathedrals appearing throughout their newly conquered lands. Canterbury had the first Norman Cathedral and Castle, with Rochester a close second. Although, many castles were built in Britain in this period each county had just one cathedral... except Kent, which is the only county in Britain to have had two cathedrals splitting the county into two dioceses.

During the medieval period Canterbury became by charter a *county corporate*. i.e. a town with rights to act like a county. The City and Borough of Canterbury which covered some surrounding villages was administered independently of the county of Kent between 1471 and 1972. Hence there were two county assizes at Canterbury and Maidstone and each has a County Court in use today.

Invicta Unconquered

There are several versions of this legend. The following was written in a thirteenth century chronicle by Thomas Sprot a monk of St. Augustine's Abbey Canterbury. Sprot describes the gathering at Swanscombe of the Men of East Kent with their Saxon Archbishop Stigand of Canterbury. They were awaiting

King William I, the Conqueror, who was taking his first journey through Kent; after the Battle of Hastings and his coronation in Westminster Abbey on Christmas Day 1066.

On his way to Dover to take ship to his lands in Normandy he was prevented from passing into the lands of East Kent by a deputation of the Men of Kent. They held a branch [treaty] or a sword [war] and told William to choose. The legend suggests that he chose the branch and in doing so agreed that the people of both East and West Kent could keep certain rights and customs if in return they would accept him as their King. Reputedly this is why the custom of Gavelkind continued in Kent centuries after vanishing from other parts of England.

Gavelkind

Gavelkind (in a nutshell) was a system whereby a deceased person's land and assets were shared amongst their heirs. It did not entirely preclude women unlike primogeniture; where assets usually went to the eldest son or nearest male relative. In many cases primogeniture effectively debarred even a closely related female from inheriting whilst a male relative could be found; notwithstanding the remoteness of his claim and the closeness of hers! Even so, there are a few cases of women inheriting titles, lands and wealth. Joan the Fair Maid of Kent (wife of the Black Prince) was Countess of Kent suo jure (in her own right). As her brother had no male relatives when he died Joan inherited everything.

Gavelkind was not abolished until The Law of Property Act 1925.

Invicta - Kent's white horse

The emblem of Kent and also of Kent Family History Society, traditionally it is shown on a red background. In 2017, as part of a rebranding exercise, Kent FHS reverted to this traditional style. The horse is affectionately named after his Latin motto *Invicta* meaning *unconquered*. A reminder that Kent was not conquered at Hastings on 14 October 1066.

Kent today

After the 1972 reorganisation of English counties Canterbury came under County administration. Kent County Council then administered almost the entire county. However, the united county was to last less than thirty years as in 1998 the Unitary Authority of Medway was formed from Rochester, Chatham, Gillingham and Strood and the county was once again split in two.

Kent Travel Guide
Abbeys and Monasteries in Kent
Aylesford Priory (The Friars)

Aylesford, Kent, England, ME20 7BX
The medieval Great Courtyard and Pilgrim's Hall, dated to 1280.

The First Carmelite House

In 1242 Richard de Grey granted land along the River Medway close to his manor at Aylesford to a group of Carmelite friars from the Holy Land. In 1247 the Archbishop of Rochester officially recognised the Aylesford Carmelites, and the first church for the newly established order was dedicated the following year.

The early Carmelites had been hermits, but they now became mendicants, meaning they could not own property and relied on begging or charitable donations.

To say that the order flourished would be an understatement; over the next 50 years over 30 Carmelite friaries were established in England and Wales, including in large centres like Cambridge, Oxford, and London.

The order at Aylesford was well supported, and built a range of guesthouses for pilgrims and established a fine library. A fine new church was built to replace the older chapel, but though it was blessed in 1348 it was not actually consecrated until 1417.

Why the wait? Well, 1348 was the year the Black Death, or bubonic plague, came to England, and we can only assume that the Carmelites of Aylesford, like the rest of the country, were badly affected by the scourge.

St Simon Stock's Vision
In the middle of the 13th century St Simon Stock, Prior General of the Carmelites, is said to have had a religious vision in which Our Lady appeared to him and promised that all who wore the Carmelite habit would have her protection.

Traditions differ on whether the vision occurred at Aylesford or Cambridge, but in any event the wearing of the Carmelite scapular became popular, especially in the 16th century.

However, the golden age at Aylesford could not survive the winds of religious change, and the abbey was dissolved by Henry VIII in the Reformation. The king granted the Priory buildings to Sir Thomas Wyatt, but the Wyatt family lost the estates under Queen Mary, and Aylesford was later granted to Sir John Sedley, who converted the monastic buildings into a luxurious mansion. In 1633 the Sedley's sold Aylesford to Sir Peter Rycaut, a Royalist supporter who used the buildings to store arms during the Civil War.

The Rycaut's suffered for their Royalist beliefs and his wife was forced to sell Aylesford once more, to Sir John Banks, a wealthy businessman. Banks rebuilt the mansion in Caroline style and welcomed the great and good of Restoration society to his new home, including Samuel Pepys, who noted in his diary that 'I was mighty pleased with the sight of it'. Banks' daughter Elizabeth married Heneage Finch, who was named 1st Earl of Aylesford, but the family lived elsewhere and used Ayesford purely as a dower house.

A subsequent owner was a Mrs Woolsey, who actively promoted the new scouting movement, and Lord Baden-Powell, the founder of the Boy Scouts, was a known visitor.

Then in 1949, an extraordinary twist of fate, the house was put up for sale, and the Carmelite order was able to buy it. Now called 'The Friars' (a name that was also used well back in the Middle Ages), the priory was restored and many of the original medieval features brought back to light from under centuries of later building.

The centrepiece of the restored Priory was an open air shrine with a series of smaller chapels leading off the open space. The 'new' Aylesford Priory was (re)dedicated in 1965. It now serves as a retreat and conference centre, and welcomes residential visitors and tourists.

Peace Garden
One of the most recent additions at Aylesford Priory is a narrow walled garden extending from the 16th-century gatehouse. The gatehouse was built for defence, guarding the entrance to the site when the priory was a mansion following the Dissolution. The garden is laid out along a walkway paved with stones bearing the word 'peace' in over 300 languages.

Rosary Way
A leafy trail along the River Medway, leading a shrine depicting St Simon Stock's scapular vision. It is amazing to think that hundreds of thousands of pilgrims have walked this same trail over the centuries.

Main Shrine And Chapels
This area is centred on a large piazza with long benches. Several shrines are laid out around the piazza, including a Choir Chapel, Cloister Chapel, St Joseph's Chapel, and the Main Shrine, with a huge sculpture of the Virgin Mary sculpted by Michael Clark in

1960. The most interesting building from a historical viewpoint is the Relic Chapel, which houses a reliquary containing the skull of St Simon Stock. Many of the chapels feature quite stunning ceramics by Polish artist Adam Kossowski.

Great Courtyard And Pilgrim's Hall

The oldest part of The Friars; most of the buildings are medieval, though many were refitted with 17th-century windows. The most intriguing is Pilgrim's Hall, dating to 1280, the hall has served many functions over its lifetime, being a barn, a brewhouse, an almshouse, and a Scout headquarters.

Visiting The Friars

I was of two minds whether to visit The Friars or not, simply because I wasn't sure how I'd enjoy a historic site that has been so recently rebuilt. But I loved it. The core of historic buildings is quite wonderful, and the restoration is so sensitively done that it was frankly hard to tell which bits were old and which bits weren't! More tellingly, the whole site seemed to radiate a sense of peace and calm, despite occasional noise from the nearby M20.

The River Medway flows past the site as it has done for almost 800 years, giving me a sense of what it might have been like for the medieval friars and pilgrims who came here. The Great

Courtyard is an absolute gem; a wonderfully complete and atmospheric medieval enclave of historic buildings.

Eastbridge Hospital of St Thomas

25 High Street, Canterbury, Kent, England, CT1 2BD

Established in the 12th century by the Archbishop of Canterbury as a place of hospitality to pilgrims, Eastbridge Hospital has operated as an almshouse for the last 400 years. View the Gothic undercoft, Pilgrims Chapel, and see the Refectory with its 13th-century wall paintings.

History

Pilgrims began descending in large numbers on Canterbury in the decades immediately following the murder of Thomas Becket in 1170. So many pilgrims, in fact, that Edward FitzOsbern was moved to establish St Thomas Hospital on the East Bridge on Canterbury's busy High Street. This new foundation was not a hospital in the modern sense, but a place where pilgrims could find accommodation and meals while staying in Canterbury to visit Becket's shrine.

The link to Becket did not stop there, for the first Master of the Hospital was probably Becket's nephew, Ralph.

The Hospital declined over the next century or so until it was re-founded in 1324 by Bishop Stratford. The next century saw St Thomas's prosper, and at the time of Chaucer's Canterbury Tales it was at the height of its wealth. The Master of Eastbridge Hospital was not just responsible for running the Hospital, he also had to maintain East Bridge itself.

The Dissolution of the Monasteries indirectly affected St Thomas, when Becket's shrine was destroyed and the number of pilgrims dropped. In 1569 a school was established at the Hospital, and this continued for almost 300 years. Then in 1584, an act of Parliament changed St Thomas's remit completely; it was ordered to offer accommodation for 10 poor residents of Canterbury and to provide a dole payment to 10 more.

The Eastbridge Hospital still continues as an almshouse to this day and houses elderly people with a strong connection to Canterbury. The Hospital also maintains nearby Greyfriars Chapel.

Lesnes Abbey

Lesnes Abbey is a 12th-century monastery founded because of a guilty conscience. The ruins of this medieval Augustinian abbey stand near the south bank of the River Thames, near a popular nature reserve on the eastern fringes of suburban London.

History

After the Norman Conquest of 1066 the estate of Lesnes was owned by Bishop Odo, half-brother of William the Conqueror and one of the most powerful men in Norman England.

Lesnes Abbey was founded by Richard de Luci in 1178. De Luci (or de Lucy) was Chief Justiciar of England under Henry II (roughly the medieval equivalent of the Prime Minister) and he may have founded the abbey in repentance for his role in the murder of Thomas Becket. The official dedication was the Abbey of St Mary and St Thomas the Martyr, which lends credence to the idea that de Luci was suffering from guilt over his involvement in Becket's murder.

The new monastery followed the Augustinian rule, and the first canons came from Holy Trinity, Aldgate, in London. De Luci resigned from office just a year after he founded the abbey, and retired to Lesnes where he died just a few months later. He was buried in the abbey's chapter house.

The founder's great-granddaughter, Roesia of Dover, was raised at Lesnes, and though she moved away to marry, she requested that her heart be buried at the abbey after her death. You can see a plaque marking the site of her heart burial in a side chapel of the high altar area of the abbey church.

In 1381, during the turmoil of the Peasant's Revolt, a mob led by Abel Ker, a former soldier and resident of Erith, broke into the abbey and forced the abbot to swear an oath that he supported their cause. After he gave in to their demands they marched off to join the main 'army' marching on London.

The abbot of Lesnes was one of the largest landowners in the area, so he took a major role in draining the nearby marshes. He was also responsible for keeping the riverside embankments in good repair, and the combined cost helped keep the abbey in serious financial trouble for long periods. A visitation in the 14th century found many of the monastic buildings in a poor state of repair.

The abbey never grew to any great size and became one of the first monastic houses suppressed by Cardinal Wolsey on behalf of Henry VIII in 1525. At that time the abbey sustained just 5 canons under an Abbot. Wolsey granted the estate to his new foundation of Cardinal's College, Oxford (now Christ Church College). The monastic buildings were destroyed except for the

Abbot's own lodging, which served as a mansion for the manor of Lesnes. The rest of the site was robbed for building materials and the abbot's house was incorporated into a farmhouse.

In 1633 the last private owner of the monastic lands, Thomas Hawes, left the estate to Christ's Hospital in London in his will.

In 1930 London County Council bought the site and opened it to the public as a park. In 1986 control passed to the London Borough of Bexley.

Lesnes is home to a mulberry tree purchased by King James I in the early 17th century. The king was ken to establish a silk industry and reportedly planted some 30,000 mulberry trees. What the king and his advisors did not realise is that silk moths feed on the leaves of white mulberry trees, and the trees they purchased were black mulberry, so the whole project was a spectacular failure.

Only the foundations remain today of this scheduled ancient monument, but they give an idea of what this small abbey near the Thames must have been like. One odd feature is that the abbey church stood on the south side of the cloisters rather than the usual north. This may be because of the sloping site, with marshy ground close to the river.

Walls stand to a height of 2.5m (about 9 feet high) and are built from a mix of flint, chalk, and Kentish ragstone. The most obvious part of the ruins is the abbey church, which is laid out on a cruciform plan with the nave measuring 70m x 22m and the transepts 43m x 19m. The west range boasts foundations of a brewhouse, kitchen, and cellarer's store, while to the north is the frater. The east range includes a sacristy, parlour, chapter house, dorter undercroft, and warming house while in an extension to the north is the reredorter and abbot's lodging. To the east stands a separate infirmary.

Opposite the abbey ruins is a recreated Monk's Garden, built on the site of the post-medieval farm. The garden features plants that the medieval monks would have cultivated for their medicinal properties. Plants such as rue, rosemary, dill, chamomile, hyssop, and sage were used in a variety of treatments including infusions and poultices for maladies from indigestion to muscle aches. Rue could also be used as a holy water sprinkler during exorcism ceremonies.

Abbey Woods
The abbey site gives access to a large area of woodland known as Lesnes Abbey Wood, created from the medieval monastic parkland. There are bluebell woods, ornamental gardens, formal

terraces, and self-guided nature trails through a network of paths across the site.

Getting There

Lesnes Abbey is extremely easy to reach from central London. Take the train from London Bridge rail station to Abbey Wood. There are regular services throughout the day and the journey is quite short - approximately 27 minutes depending on the time of day. Depending on when you read this you can also take the Elizabeth Line from Canary Wharf and it will take just 12 minutes. From the station entrance turn sharp right and take the stairs down to street level.

Go straight up Wilton Road and take the first left onto Abbey Road, which takes you under the A2041 overpass. Take the second right onto New Road and you will see the entrance to Abbey Wood on your left. From the park entrance just follow the footpath past the cafe at the top of the hill and you will see the abbey ruins immediately beyond. From the rail station, it takes no more than 10 minutes easy walk to reach the abbey.

If you are coming from outside London, the abbey lies about 8 miles from Junction 2 of the M25. Be aware that it isn't terribly well signposted and there is no dedicated parking area.

Editor's Soapbox

I'm astonished that Lesnes Abbey isn't better known. The abbey ruins are easily as impressive as many more popular medieval monasteries, and it is an absurdly easy place to reach from central London. Maybe it is the fact that it lies in a London suburb, but it seems really odd that more people don't know about - or visit - this very well-preserved site.

To be sure, there are no soaring arches; little has survived of the abbey church, which must have been extremely impressive in its day. Most of the ruins are no more than foundation walls, though some walls still stand well over head height and there are several very nicely-preserved doorways and windows.

Minster Abbey, Minster-in-Thanet

History

The roots of Minster Abbey go back to a 7th-century crime. Two brothers, members of the Mercian royal family, were staying at the court of their uncle, King Egbert of Kent. The brothers fell afoul of court intrigue and were murdered. Their elder sister, Queen Ermenburga of Mercia, came to Kent to claim the customary *weregild*, or compensation fee offered to the family of a murdered man. With Ermenburga came her two young daughters, Mildred and Milgitha.

Ermenburga's Deer

Now, instead of simply taking the weregild 'blood money', Ermenburga asked Egbert for land to found a monastery. The contrite Egbert agreed, but according to legend, put a condition upon the gift. For it seems that Ermenburga owned a pet deer, which she brought with her to Kent.

Egbert agreed to donate land on the Isle of Thanet, with the boundary to be determined by the course the deer took if left to wander across the island on its own. In those days Thanet was a large island, cut off from the Kentish mainland by a wide channel, stretching from Reculver in the north to Richborough on the south coast. The deer was duly released and took a wandering path across Thanet which eventually took in a huge amount of land in the south of the island.

The lands between the deer's course and the Wentsum Channel was then awarded by Egbert to the newly founded abbey at Minster. The modern chapel at Minster Abbey recalls this tale; there is a large and very striking carving of Ermenburga and her deer on the side of the building.

The first monastery was built where the large medieval parish church now stands, several hundred yards away from the current abbey grounds, but perfectly placed for a natural harbour which led into the Wentsum Channel. It was the harbour that led to Minster's prosperity over the ensuing centuries, allowing grain from Kent to be shipped to London.

Minster Abbey was consecrated in 670 by St Theodore, then Archbishop of Canterbury. The first abbess was Ermenburga, who had taken the name Domna Eva on taking vows. Domna Eva's daughter Mildred later joined the abbey as well.

When Domna Eva retired in 690, Mildred became abbess of Minster. The new abbess was famed for her generosity to the poor and was a well-loved figure in the area. She died in 725AD, but even 3 centuries later, in 1097 the chronicler Goscelin called her 'the fairest lily of the English'. She was eventually beatified as St Mildred in 1388.

By 741AD the abbey had outgrown its original buildings, with about 70 nuns having joined the community. So the 3rd abbess, St Edburga, decided to build new monastic buildings a short distance away, on the site of the present abbey. These 8th-century buildings were of timber, probably topped by thatch, or lead roofs.

A new chapel was erected, dedicated to St Peter and St Paul. Under the leadership of Edburga, Minster supported missionary work in Europe, particularly that of St Boniface in Germany. The kings of Kent added more land to the original abbey estates, and under Edburga Minster eventually controlled fully half of Thanet.

The Arrival Of The Danes

But this period of growth and prosperity was not to continue, and in the late 8th century the Danes appeared in the longboats, bent on plunder. The first Danish raid was recorded in AD 753, but the Danes were a constant threat for the next 2 centuries and more.

In 797 the fifth abbess, Seldritha, took over, but her efforts to rebuild the abbey's fortunes were dealt an ultimately fatal blow in 840 when the Danes burned Minster to the ground and killed the entire monastic community of nuns and servants.

With the death of the nuns, the monastic estates reverted to the kings of Kent, and the monastery was finished.

Or was it?

A Midnight Raid

In 1027, over 180 years after the final Danish raid, the monks of Canterbury petitioned King Canute to give them the abbey lands. Canute agreed, and the monks began to rebuild the earlier timber buildings in stone. But that wasn't all; they asked that the relics of St Mildred be transferred to them.

The king eventually agreed, but the townsfolk of Minster were not likely to agree to have the relics of their beloved saint taken away. One account suggests that 4 monks of Canterbury raided Mildred's tomb in the dead of night, stole the relics, and managed to make it to the ferry at Sarre before the alarmed townsfolk could catch them.

Worse was to come, for after William the Conqueror and his Normans invaded England, they laid waste to Thanet, so that if the Danes raided they would find no food or stronghold. The devastation of Thanet must have terrible for the inhabitants, and an account in 1097 says that the abbey chapel was roofless and neglected.

When the Danish threat receded the inhabitants of Thanet gradually returned, and they built dwellings on the foundations of St Mildred's monastery, and erected a church, presumably over the saint's shrine.

Over the next few decades, the abbey was gradually rebuilt and expanded by the Abbots of Canterbury. In the 12th century, a single-storey hall was added to the Saxon wing, and in 1413 both were raised to 2 storeys by Abbot Thomas Hunden of Canterbury. Abbot Hunden was also responsible for the large mullioned windows in the Saxon west wing. Abbot Hunden's monogram is engraved on the north door of the Norman wing.

The abbey was dissolved by Henry VIII in 1538, and both the church and manor became royal property. The chapel was destroyed and the monastic buildings allowed to decay. Throughout this tumultuous period, however, the north and west wings survived relatively intact. Like so many monastic sites, Minster passed through numerous hands over the following centuries. But where so many other sites around England fell into complete ruin, Minster had a different fate.

The Abbey Reborn
In 1937 a group of Benedictine nuns from southern Germany took possession of the site and established a new monastery at

Minster. They had scarcely begun to integrate themselves into local society when the Second World War broke out.

Being German, the nuns were considered a security threat by the government and the nunnery was temporarily suspended and the nuns interned for the duration of the war. In this case the internment could have been worse, for they were sent to existing British monasteries.

After the war they returned to Minster, and over the ensuing decades rebuilt the medieval buildings and added new ones. One of the most recent additions is a modern chapel, but even there the link with Minster's past is not forgotten, for the relics of St Mildred are stored in a reliquary within the chapel.

The Abbey Today
The oldest part of the abbey is the west wing, built around 1027 and restored after the Norman destruction of 1085. The distinctive Saxon herringbone stonework can still be seen, pierced by narrow rectangular windows in the east wall.

Joining the west wing is the 12th century Norman Great Hall, divided into four bays, with round-headed windows in the upper stages. When the Great Hall was built a passage was made through the Saxon wing. This vaulted passage is one of the highlights of the visitor tour, and shows traditional Norman vaulting technique and stonework, creating a very atmospheric set of low chambers.

In the 1930s excavations revealed the plan of the Norman chapel, but this is now buried under turf. However, in dry weather the outline of the foundations can be seen on the lawn.

The most obvious medieval remains are the large west tower, now a crumbling, and rather romantic, ruin. The tower probably served as a place of refuge in times of trouble, and as a lookout for Danish raiders. It was a massive structure, with buttressed corners 37 feet apart and a spiral stair built into the thickness of the north wall.

Around the side of the tower, set into a stone archway, is a medieval carving of Christ in Majesty. This carving, of a subject often used to decorate tympana over church doorways, was found in a pile of rubble by one of the post-medieval owners of the Minster estate and rescued from oblivion.

Visiting Minster Abbey
The abbey is a practising Benedictine community, but there are regular, free tours of the site (check the abbey website for details). I was fortunate enough to attend one of the tours and I

found it a delight. The very friendly guide told us about the history of the site, the establishment of the 7th-century nunnery, and the personalities involved. She showed us into the vaulted Norman passage under the Saxon wing and took us around the tower to look at the medieval tympanum carving.

We were able to explore the chapel, but not the Norman wing, as that is still in use by the nuns. The tour was short, about 30 minutes, but extremely enjoyable, and gave me a real appreciation for the rich history of the site, which has one of the oldest buildings in England still in use. The abbey is set in quite wonderful gardens, and seems a veritable oasis of calm; quite a contrast to the turbulent history of this ancient site.

About Minster Abbey

Address: *Church Street, Minster-in-Thanet, Kent, England, CT12 4BX*

Attraction Type: Abbey

Location: The abbey entrance is at the junction of Church Street and Bedlam Court Lane. For satnav use the postcode CT12 4HF

St Augustine's Abbey

In this case the abbey isn't just dedicated to St. Augustine, it was actually founded by him, in AD 598, to house the monks he brought with him to convert the Britons to Christianity.

Shortly after Augustine's arrival in 597 King Ethelbert of Kent granted him a parcel of land stretching to about 30 acres (18 hectares) outside the walls of the city, near the course of the main road to the coast. In 598 Augustine established a monastic settlement with the small group of monks who had accompanied him to Kent. The abbey lands probably included St Martin's church, an existing Romano-British church where Bertha, Ethelbert's Frankish wife, already worshipped.

The abbey was used as a burial place for kings of Kent and the first archbishops of Canterbury (the archbishops were later within the cathedral itself). The site used for the burials of kings can still be seen amid the abbey ruins.

When the abbey was built, one of Augustine's companions, named Peter, was elected as the first official abbot of the new monastery. That first abbey included domestic buildings, about which little is known. It also included a linear row of chapels, in a style then common on the European continent. One of the first chapels was the little brick church of St Pancras. The remains of this chapel can be seen at the furthest end of the abbey grounds from the visitor centre. A theory has been put forward that St Pancras was the church established by Queen Bertha, rather than St Martin's. St Pancras is certainly a very early church, and uses Roman bricks extensively.

There was a school attached to the abbey (or possibly at the cathedral). This school, which may well have been established by Augustine himself, quickly began to draw scholars from across Britain, and by the late 7th century the school had attained a reputation as a place of learning. There was also a library, which included books brought by Augustine, and more sent by Pope Gregory.

The abbey was reorganised by Dunstan, Archbishop from 959 to follow the current reforms in Benedictine rule. Abbey buildings were expanded and the church rebuilt. The early dedication of the abbey was not to Augustine, but to SS Peter and Paul. Dunstan changed that; when his rebuilt church was finished he rededicated it to St Augustine and Peter and Paul. From that point it became popularly known as St Augustine's.

Abbot Wulfric (1047-59) was responsible for the most striking feature of the monastery ruins that still survives. This is the octagonal rotunda built to link the church of St Peter and Paul with the chapel dedicated to St Mary.

The first Norman abbot, Scolland, rebuilt many of the monastic buildings in Romanesque style. When Scolland died, the Archbishop of Canterbury named his successor, despite the objections of the monks. Several of the monks were arrested (see Canterbury Castle entry) and the objections died down quickly. The rebuilding of the Saxon abbey buildings continued until the end of the 12th century.

Throughout the medieval period St Augustine's Abbey built up estates throughout Kent. Included in the estates was land in Thanet granted by King Cnut. At the fullest extent of its power the abbey held over 12,000 acres of land. But that power did not last, and like all other monastic houses in the land, St Augustine's suffered at the hands of Henry VIII. On 30 July 1538 the last abbot and monks left the abbey, signalling the end of over 940 years of monastic presence.

Of the famous library, only 200 books survive, and of the abbey plate only a single silver-rimmed cup survives, in the treasury of the cathedral. After the monastery was dissolved by Henry VIII part of the abbey buildings were converted into a royal residence, used as a stopover place on journeys between London and the south coast.

The abbey site was leased out to a succession of noble families. Among these were Lord and Lady Wotton, who rented the site in 1610. The Wotton's engaged John Tradescant the Elder to lay out formal gardens within the abbey grounds. Over the subsequent centuries parts of the abbey were sold off. Some were adapted for use by King's School, the exclusive school established by Henry VIII.

By far the best surviving feature of the medieval abbey is the great 14th century gatehouse, sometimes called Fyndon's Gate. Within the grounds the most impressive remain is the north wall of the nave of the abbey church, which still stands to a great height. Abutting this is a partial wall of the Ethelbert Tower. More interesting, though, is the circular remain of Abbot Wulfric's rotunda, built around 1050.

The abbey makes up part of the Canterbury World Heritage Site, which also includes Canterbury Cathedral and the nearby church of St Martin's, the oldest church in Britain still in use.

Castles in Kent

Canterbury Castle

Address: Castle Street, Canterbury, Kent, England, CT1 2PR

When William the Conqueror overcame King Harold and his Saxons at the Battle of Hastings, one of his first acts was to establish three powerful castles in the southeast of his new realm, at Canterbury, Dover, and Rochester. His new castle at Canterbury is what is now called Dane John, a corruption of the French word for donjon, or keep.

The castle saw the first in a long line of historical dramas in 1087 when monks of St Augustine's Abbey refused to accept a new Norman abbot. Lanfranc, the Archbishop of Canterbury, had the ringleaders of the monks imprisoned in the castle and the others expelled.

The new keep was begun in the reign of William II and completed about 1120 by Henry I. This stolid stone structure stood 80 feet high and measured about 98 by 85 feet. The walls were massively thick, about 13 feet in places, and the building could only be entered by a stone stair to a first-floor door on the northwest side. The first floor had a great hall and kitchen. Below this was a basement, originally used only for storage, but later adapted to use as a dungeon.

In 1216 Louis, Dauphin of France, captured Canterbury Castle but later retreated. In 1277 Jewish citizens of Canterbury were held in the castle before being expelled from England as part of Edward I's policy. In 1303 a group of 23 prisoners who were being held for murder were released on condition that they join the king's fleet in Scotland and returned to face trial after the conflict was over.

In 1380 Wat Tyler's rebellion raised the peasants and townsfolk of Kent and the southeast. A mob stormed the castle and forced the constable to publically burn financial and legal records and release prisoners. There was further discord during the Reformation when Henry VIII's advisor, Thomas Cromwell, had two priests held at the castle for '*permitting the Bishop of Rome's name in their books*'.

But that was nothing to what was to follow. Henry's daughter, Queen Mary, had 42 people imprisoned at Canterbury Castle and put to death for their refusal to follow her Catholic faith. But we're getting ahead of ourselves ....

After Henry II built his new castle at Dover, Canterbury Castle declined in importance and became used primarily as a prison, under the control of the Sheriff of Kent. By the 13th century, a new ground-level gate was created on the south-east side.

By the 17th century, the castle had fallen into ruin. In 1609 James I granted it to Sir Anthony Weldon, and in 1730 a new County Session House was built on the site of the medieval great hall.

In 1825 the castle was used by the Canterbury Gas Light and Coke Company as a storage depot for coal and coke, and later a large water tank was set up on the ruins of the keep. In 1901 the castle was described as '*a most miserable discoloured ruin, its Cyclopean walls begrimed with soot and filth.*' Thankfully the castle was purchased by Canterbury City Council, who have restored it to its current condition.

The builders of the keep walls made heavy use of old Roman tiles and bricks, in addition to local flint. Note the decorated courses of the walls; these are made from Quarr stone, a distinctive stone from the Isle of Wight. Stores of Quarr were depleted by the 12th century and can only be found in early Norman buildings.

Near the southwest corner of the keep is a small section of the 3rd-century Roman town wall.

Little remains in the interior, though the foundations of inner chambers can be seen, and the recesses which held the floor timbers. One tower stair still rises to the full height of the castle, allowing excellent views of the interior and across the city.

Dane John Mound

Dane John Mound is a conical hill that was the site of one of the first Norman motte and bailey castles erected by William the Conqueror. Archaeological excavation has revealed that the mound was a Roman burial site on the line of the old Roman city walls.

The Normans merely adapted the existing mound as a good spot to erect a fortification. That early motte and bailey castle was later superseded by the stone fortress of Canterbury Castle a short distance away.

Around 1790 Alderman James Simmons laid out a formal garden around the foot of the castle mound. He also laid out a winding path to the top of the mound, where there now stands a white stone obelisk in his honour.

The name Dane John is generally assumed to be an English corruption of 'donjon', a term for a defensive structure or

Norman keep. Another explanation is that the name was invented by a 17th-century antiquarian who theorized that the mound was erected by Danes.

Visitors can walk along the old city walls from the castle mound. Several of the surviving towers, such as nearby Whitecross Tower, have interpretation panels giving insights into the history of the tower and the town defences.

Address: *Castle Row, Watling Street, Canterbury, Kent, England, CT1 1YW*

Deal Castle

Severe concentric semi-circular towers rise up like a flattened stone wedding cake at Deal Castle, one of Henry VIII's string of coastal castles built against the threat of a French invasion. Built to take advantage of the new super-weapon, cannons, Deal boasts 119 gun positions.

History

When Francis I, King of France, signed an alliance with the Holy Roman Emperor, Charles V, in 1538, Henry VIII's England was threatened by the combined might of the two European super-powers of the day. Henry's foreign policy had relied on playing off France and the Empire against each other, but an alliance between the two put England under immediate threat.

Henry's response to launch a huge building project, erecting a series of forts along the English coast; the largest such coastal defence project since the Romans built a series of Saxon-shore forts over 1000 years previously.

Deal was one of Henry's new forts, the largest along the Kent coast, and it remains the best-preserved, giving us a unique insight into life in Tudor England. It may seem surprising that Henry should build a fort at Deal; in fact, he built 3 forts within 2 miles, the others being at Sandown (now destroyed) and Walmer.

The reason was that the area around Deal offered easy landing to an invasion force. To counter this possibility Henry linked the three new forts with an earthwork interspersed with bastions. The earthworks are long gone, but the Henrican forts at Walmer and Deal remain.

One of the challenges for Henry and his military engineers was how to counter the threat of cannon, the 16th-century equivalent of a nuclear bomb.

Traditional medieval castle structures, with their high, thick walls, and rectangular towers, would not stand up to a bombardment of cannon-fire. Henry's designers also needed to give the castle garrison opportunity to use their own artillery to maximum impact.

The solution, probably engineered by Stefan von Haschenperg, was a concentric fortress, with a series of curving walls in a flower pattern, overlapped to provide firing angles, with the curve of the walls lessening the damage of a direct hit from enemy fire.

At the centre was a low, sturdy tower, surrounded by a series of six semi-circular bastions, encircled by a ditch and a curtain wall with six projecting lobes. Cannon were mounted at each level, allowing simultaneous firing from the tower, inner bastions, and outer bastions.

The fort was set down low to the ground, thus giving the enemy less to fire at. The fact that the final result looked similar to a Tudor rose symbol probably played a part in the design process, but the main reason for the design was purely practical.

The core of the building is brick, faced with stone throughout. There are quarters for the garrison and governor in the central tower, with a spiral stair joining the levels. From the basement level, a pair of corridors run to a fighting gallery in the curtain wall.

The threat posed by France and Spain never came; perhaps Henry's coastal defences played a deterrent role, but we shall never know for certain. The Spanish Armada passed close to Deal, but by that time the Armada was already in disarray and posed no threat.

The only military action at Deal came during the Civil War, when Royalists took control of all three forts during an abortive 1648 uprising in favour of Charles II. They were only ousted with great difficulty. The castle was manned in the Napoleonic Wars, but again saw no action.

Visiting Deal Castle

The castle is very well signposted, so there's no problem finding it! We visited on a blistering hot summer day, when the heat bounced up off the dry stone walls and cobbled courtyard, and made it a relief to dive into the passages inside the central tower. It really won't take too long to explore the site; it is perhaps easier to think of Deal as a fort rather than a castle, like, say, Dover Castle further along the coast.

I would allow from 30 minutes to 1 hour to see the entire site. Though Deal is not as immediately impressive as Dover, it was never intended to fulfil the same purpose. It is fascinating for what it is; a wonderfully well-preserved example of a Tudor coastal fort with an innovative design that was, in its day, state-of-the-art.

Dover Castle

Underground tunnels begun by King John, later used in WWII

Dover Castle was begun in 1066 but is largely a product of Henry II's expansion in 1170. In the 13th century, King John ordered the building of underground tunnels connected to sally ports in order to surprise attacking troops. These tunnels were later used as a military command centre during WWII (see the extensive reconstructions). Within the castle grounds stand a Roman lighthouse and a Saxon church.

History
'The Key to the Kingdom'

This imposing castle towers - quite literally - over the historic port of Dover, at the western end of the iconic White Cliffs. The Iron Age inhabitants of the area we now call Kent recognised the strategic importance of the hill, and built a fort here over 2000 years ago.

The Romans, in turn, built a pharos, or lighthouse, inside the hill fort, and a matching lighthouse atop the Western Heights, across Dover harbour. The second lighthouse is gone now, but the first one still stands atop the hill looking across to France, 21 miles away.

Long after the Romans left in AD 410 a Saxon burgh, or fortified town, flourished within the earthwork defences. Around AD 1000 the Saxons erected a church beside the Roman lighthouse. The church of St Mary in Castro still stands, though much remodelled in the Victorian period.

According to legend, King Harold, the last Saxon king of England, promised to give Dover 'castle' to William the Conqueror. It seems doubtful that there was anything resembling an actual castle at that time, and Harold may simply have meant the fortified hilltop and Iron Age defences.

William marched through Dover following his success at the Battle of Hastings in 1066, and built a ringwork defensive wall, much of which is obliterated by later construction. Sometime in the century following the Norman invasion the town of Dover moved from the hilltop to the low-lying land by the harbour.

Whether this move was voluntary or enforced by the Normans we simply don't know, but when Henry II decided to create his magnificent new stone castle here in 1080 the hilltop site was largely empty aside from the church and lighthouse. Henry built a huge stone keep, protected by a ringwork inner curtain wall to the north-west of the original ringwork.

We know from the Royal Pipe Rolls, or financial records, that from 1080-1090 the crown spent 6300 pounds building Dover Castle. For the time this was an eye-watering amount of money, and underlines just how imposing and impressive Henry meant his new fortress to be.

Unusually for the period, we even know the name of the builder; the king's Master Mason, one Maurice the Engineer, who had just completed the castle keep at Newcastle-upon-Tyne.

King John extended Henry II's outer curtain wall, starting work in 1207 after he had lost control of Normandy. He must have sensed a threat from France, and he was right, though not perhaps in quite the way he might have thought. For John's rebellious barons invited Louis, Dauphin of France, to become king of England.

Louis besieged Dover in 1216, digging a mine under John's gatehouse. The Constable, Hubert de Burgh, hurriedly placed timber in the breach and managed to hold off the attackers long enough for fate to take a hand.

And fate did indeed take a hand, for John conveniently died, Louis' bid for the throne faltered, and Dover was saved. The tower was rebuilt, but the gateway blocked permanently.

One of the most impressive remaining towers is Constable's Gate, so-called because it served as the official residence for the Constable after that officer moved from the first floor of the keep.

Though the curtain wall and towers might have been enough to defend Dover, the medieval engineers were not done. They built a series of underground tunnels, connecting the castle with the earthwork beyond the north curtain wall.

These tunnels, though enlarged and extended in the Napoleonic Wars, still exist in their original form. Using the tunnels, the castle garrison would have been able to send a force of men under the curtain and attack a besieging enemy from the rear.

The castle was under attack again in 1263, when Henry III's barons, led by Simon de Montfort, rebelled. De Montfort seized Dover Castle in July of that year, and in May 1264 Prince Edward (the future Edward I) was held prisoner here. De Montfort's wife, Eleanor, held the castle briefly, but when the rebel cause ended with defeat at Evesham in 1265 she was forced to surrender.

The Post-Medieval Period
Edward IV renovated Dover Castle to serve as an occasional royal residence, inserting fine new windows and fireplaces. We don't know if Edward ever actually stayed here, but other royals certainly did; in 1520 Emperor Charles V stayed in the castle, and Henry VIII stopped here on his way to the Field of the Cloth of Gold.

Henry's daughter, Elizabeth I visited, but by the time Henrietta Maria of France stayed on her way to marry Charles I, it was described as 'an old building in the antique manner'.

George de Villiers, 1st Duke of Buckingham, embarked on a lavish renovation of the Great Tower, but much of his rebuilding has been lost to time.

The castle was briefly held by Royalist troops during the Civil War, but Parliamentary supporters from the town staged a daring raid, scaling the cliffs at night and taking the garrison by surprise.

Dover escaped the slighting that Parliament meted out to so many other fortresses, but it could not escape the ravages of time; in the late 17th century the Great Tower was stripped of its creature comforts and used to house French prisoners of war. Graffiti carved into the walls by the prisoners can still be seen in places.

During the mid-18th century the defences were upgraded to counter the threat of invasion following the War of Austrian Succession (begun 1740) and the Seven Years War (1756). But the threat of invasion was far greater in the Napoleonic Wars (1793-1815) and this period saw the greatest rebuilding at Dover since the 13th century.

Much of the work was supervised by Lieutenant-Colonel William Twiss, a military engineer of outstanding ability, who built new barracks and casements, and rebuilt the walls to withstand modern artillery fire.

More impressively perhaps, Twiss built a complex of tunnels under the castle, extending to the very face of the White Cliffs. The last major building of the 19th century was the Officer's New Barracks, designed by Anthony Salvin (beside the current parking area).

The tunnels built by Twiss during the Napoleonic period were put to use during World War II, when they formed a naval operation centre and hospital. It was from here, far beneath ground level, that Vice-Admiral Bertrand Ramsay oversaw Operation Dynamo, the 'Miracle of Dunkirk' (more details below).

During the Cuban Missile Crisis of 1962, when it seemed the world might be on the brink of a nuclear war, a series of tunnels were equipped to serve as an emergency government headquarters. It was not until the 1980s that the 'nuclear' tunnels were decommissioned. Since then Dover Castle has been preserved for its historic interest and administered by English Heritage.

What to See

Arthur's Hall
Within the inner curtain, facing the Great Tower forebuilding is this great hall, the social hub of castle life, probably built for

Henry III around 1236. We do not know for certain why it is called Arthur's Hall; we can only speculate that the name was intended to honour King Arthur.

At the south-east end are three arched openings. The arches give access to the kitchens, buttery, and pantry. The hall was reroofed in the 1740s when a new floor was inserted.

Today the hall houses an exhibition on the history of the castle and the Plantagenet dynasty. Beside Arthur's Hall is the museum of the Princess of Wales Royal Regiment and the Queens Regiment.

The Medieval Tunnels

When Hubert de Burgh rebuilt the castle after the siege of 1216-17, he erected a series of outworks to the northwest of the Norfolk Towers. The new defences included the cylindrical tower of St John, in the outer ditch, and a triangular outer spur, or bastion.

From the air these early 13th century defences look like a pointed arrow projecting from the castle walls. But not all of Hubert de Burgh's work is visible above ground, for he linked his new defences to the main castle by a series of tunnels.

One shaft led beneath the Norfolk Gates to St John's Tower, where a drawbridge gave access to another tunnel under the spur. Sally ports (small side gates) gave access to the ditch. Much of the medieval tunnel system still exists, and is reached from a stair between the King's Gate and the Norfolk Gates.

The tunnels were extended and strengthened in 1756 and again in the Napoleonic War period, but they are essentially as they would have looked when they were finished in 1221, and represent an extraordinary feat of medieval engineering.

The Great Tower
The showpiece of Dover, the great stone keep erected by Maurice the Engineer for Henry II is a huge cube, measuring 100 feet in each direction, with imposing corner turrets and an elaborate L-shaped forebuilding with a further three projecting turrets.

The forebuilding acts as a grand staircase, giving access, not to the first floor, as you might expect, but to the second floor, where the royal hall and solar (private apartments) are located.

The forebuilding was originally roofless, so any attackers getting inside would be subjected to a rain of missiles thrown from the tower parapets above. At the point where the forebuilding stair changes direction there is a small, rather ornately carved chapel, perhaps erected as a place for more welcome guests to give thanks for a successful journey upon arrival.

The hall level is double-height, with a gallery running around the exterior and several small, private chambers in the thickness of the walls.

In one of these chambers is one of the most amazing - and uncelebrated - examples of medieval engineering anywhere in Britain; a well shaft, which sinks down fully 350 feet into the chalk beneath to reach water. To put that in perspective, the well shaft is as deep as the spire of Salisbury Cathedral is tall.

The main attraction in the tower, however, at least for most visitors, is that English Heritage has painstakingly recreated the look and feel of the authentic Norman castle, with bedchambers, furniture, and decoration that echo as precisely as possible what the rooms would have looked like.

The one exception to the authenticity of the decor is that there are painted wall-hangings, where the original scheme would have had the actual walls painted.

However, as one English Heritage room steward told me, they couldn't actually use paint on the walls in case they damaged the real medieval paint that still exists, so they did the next best thing. I must say that the result is staggering; every surface appears to glow with colour. It reminds me of nothing so much as a 1960s decoration scheme, with vivid, pure colours everywhere.

It is worth remembering that medieval buildings were generally highly decorated, not bare and cold stone as we so often see them today. So it is a real experience for the senses to see the rooms in the tower much as Henry II or his descendants might have seen them.

The tower is contained within an inner curtain wall with 14 mural towers. Two pairs of towers are placed close together to form the earliest twin-towered gateways in England; Palace Gate and King's Gate. Eighteenth-century barracks fill in much of the space within the inner curtain wall.

St Mary In Castro Church
This delightful cruciform church stands at the highest point of Dover Castle, its bands of red brick and pale stone standing out like a beacon. Begun around 1000 AD, and heavily remodelled in

the Victorian period, St Mary served as the church for the garrison of Dover Castle.

The size and layout of the building suggest that it was a minster, acting as a mother church for the region and served by a community of priests. Construction is of flint and ragstone rubble with Roman bricks reused in the quoins and around doors and window openings.

During the medieval period, sacred relics were kept in the church. The building was restored in 1582 but allowed to fall into decay in the 17th century.

By the 18th century, the building was little more than a crumbling shell. Used as a fives court and a coal store, the church was finally restored in 1862 by George Gilbert Scott. The final touches were applied by William Butterfield in 1888, and today the interior is typical of Butterfield's 'High Church' work, with polychrome decoration, a mosaic altar, and tiled floors.

Traditionally there were three different service times, with the rank and file attending the earliest service and higher ranks later in the day.

The Roman Lighthouse

Beside the church of St Mary stands the Roman pharos, erected to guide shipping along the coast and into Dover harbour sometime in the first half of the second century AD (i.e. roughly 125 AD).

The lighthouse is built to an octagonal plan, using ragstone and flint with brick dressings and brick archways. It is built with five tapering stages. The bottom four stages are original Roman work, while the top stage was added around 1430 by Humphrey, Duke of Gloucester, to act as a bell tower for St Mary in Castro church.

In the 1580s the lighthouse was reroofed and restored to act as a powder magazine. The structure is in remarkable condition, though obviously suffering the effects of weathering. You can go through an opening into the centre of the lighthouse, which is hollow.

Secret Wartime Tunnels
One of the most interesting - and most recent - attractions at Dover is the Secret Wartime Tunnels. These tunnels were begun during the Napoleonic Wars and greatly extended during World War II.

During that conflict they acted as the command centre for naval operations along the south coast, and it was from here that Vice-Admiral Bertrand Ramsay oversaw Operation Dynamo, the evacuation of British and Allied forces from Dunkirk.

Access to the tunnels is by guided tour only, and the tour takes about 45 minutes. It consists of a series of audio-visual experiences which tell the story of the Dunkirk rescue. At the end of the tour is a museum area, with more exhibits about the Dunkirk story and about the role played by people who worked in the tunnels during the war. There is a further tour available exploring a WWII hospital area, next to the Secret Wartime Tunnels.

From the tunnels, it is only a short walk to Admiral Ramsay's Lookout, which offers wonderful views across the Channel and east to the White Cliffs.

Visiting Dover Castle

I foolishly assumed that I could take my family around the castle in a couple of hours, and have plenty of time to see Dover itself, and pop down the coast to Deal and Walmer Castles. Oh, how wrong I was!

There is so much to see at Dover that I strongly, strongly advise you to leave at least 4 hours for a visit. If you have the time, allow 5-6 hours and take it slow and easy. There truly is so much to see that to do justice to it all you really need a minimum of a half day, and, depending on your interests, a lot more.

The wartime tunnels alone will take at least 45 minutes - more if you take your time over the museum at the end of the tour, and that's not counting the time you may have to stand in line if it is a busy time of year.

Something For Everyone
Perhaps a personal anecdote best sums up visiting Dover Castle; when my family had finished our visit (our second in 4 days!) I asked everyone which part had been their favourite. We each chose something different. My daughter liked St Mary de Castro church, my son the medieval tunnels, my wife the Great Tower, and I was torn between the Wartime Tunnels and the Roman lighthouse!

Eynsford Castle

Address: High Street, Eynsford, Kent, England, DA4 0AA

Eynsford Castle is a Norman castle of the 'enclosure' type, built roughly 1085-87 with encircling curtain walls. Most early Norman castles followed a motte and bailey plan of a wooden palisade atop a raised mound, surrounded by an enclosed bailey, or courtyard.

By contrast, Eynsford Castle consists of a simple enclosing wall around an inner cluster of buildings, reached by a drawbridge across a shallow moat. There was no central keep or tower, and all the important accommodation was on the first floor of the hall building. There was an outer bailey, or enclosure, to the south-east, but no excavations have been done in this area and we do not know what buildings might have stood there.

The castle was built in 1085-7 by William de Eynsford, who served as Sheriff of Kent. It is built on top of an earlier Saxon structure. The castle was enlarged a century later, at which time a great hall and further domestic buildings were constructed within the walls. A gatehouse was added, and the walls raised and strengthened. There was no central keep; rather, the main domestic quarters were arranged on the first floor of the hall.

There are a pair of undercrofts in the hall. One was used for storage, but the other constituted a rather posh solar; a self-contained living area complete with living quarters, garderobe, and fireplace. This separate apartment may have been used by the castle bailiff.

The hall was expanded in the 13th century with the addition of a separate forebuilding, but early in that same century, the building was badly damaged by fire. When the damage was repaired a new kitchen was built to serve the hall and private apartments.

At the far left of the site are the foundations of the well, and kitchen block, built between 1150-1175. This remained in use until the castle was abandoned after 1312. Kitchens were always kept separate from living quarters due to the risk of fire. Remains of three garderobes (latrines) can be seen built into the thickness of the walls. These would have emptied directly into the moat.

Feuding Families

The early history of Eynsford Castle was largely taken over by squabbles between the neighbouring families of Kirkeby and Criol. In 1261 the castle and estates were divided between the families, and they constantly fought over their respective rights.

In 1312 the Kirkeby's sold the castle to Judge William Inge. A band of men under Nicholas de Criol broke into Eynsford Castle and ransacked it. The castle seems to have been abandoned after this act of vandalism.

After passing through many hands the castle was purchased by the Hart Dyke family, who also owned Lullingstone Castle. The Hart Dykes used Eynsford for stabling their horses and as a kennel for their hunting dogs.

In 1835 architect Edward Cresy was brought in to clear the ancient site of modern buildings. Cresy made an extensive survey of the castle and began to rebuild the original structure. However, in 1872 a section of the curtain wall collapsed. This exposed the original Norman mound inside the wall. This can best be seen from the far (north) side of the castle enclosure, where a concrete retaining wall has been inserted to secure the site. The retaining wall has been marked to show the excavated layers of the mound.

Visiting Eynsford Castle

The castle is *technically* signposted, but honestly, you'd have to be travelling south and be looking in just the right spot to see the sign. We weren't, so we didn't (if you follow me). It took several attempts to find the small lane on the north side of the A225 that leads to a small parking area beside the castle. The entrance to the lane is almost directly opposite the Castle Hotel (a clue, I suppose).

Now that I've had my rant, let me say that I enjoyed the castle enormously. It won't take long to explore the site, but there is plenty of interest if you enjoy medieval castles. The enclosure layout is different from the more typical motte and bailey Norman plans and is rather fascinating. What makes Eynsford Castle so interesting is that the design was scarcely altered after the 12th century.

Access is by a bridge across a dry moat, leading through a ruined gatehouse area into a circular enclosure bounded by high walls on most of the site. To the left of the entrance are three large openings which were probably used as garderobes - sort of a communal privy by the look of it. At the far left are the foundations of the later kitchen, near a well-protected by iron bars.

The entire right side of the site is taken up by the ruins of the hall and kitchens. But when I say 'ruins' that might give the wrong impression; there's actually quite a lot of the hall and its subsidiary buildings still intact. That was one of the impressive features of the castle for me; that so much of the hall still stands.

You can see remains of a spiral stair in one corner, and parts of a fireplace. But the most impressive part of the castle are the walls, which are really very impressive and really emphasize just how different Eynsford is to a 'normal' Norman castle.

Hever Castle

Address: Edenbridge, Kent, England, TN8 7NG

Hever Castle is a marvellous sight; it seems to float upon the wide moat that surrounds it, and its setting within the extensive gardens is exquisite. The castle itself is approached across a drawbridge over the moat. Visitors then pass beneath the teeth of two portcullis into the inner courtyard of the castle.

The Castle

Hever Castle was begun in 1270 by William de Hever, though the gatehouse is all that remains of that early fortress. In 1462 the castle passed to the Bullen (Boleyn) family, and Geoffrey de Bullen added wings on each side of the existing gatehouse.

Several decades after the Boleyn family took over Hever, its most famous inhabitant, Anne Boleyn, was born. Anne would spend much of her childhood at Hever, and Henry VIII is known to have visited during his courtship. Anne's father, Thomas de Boleyn, expanded Hever still further, adding the Long Gallery, among other features.

After Anne's death the castle was given to Anne of Cleves, Henry's fourth wife, and in the centuries that followed it passed through the hands of several owners until in 1903 it was purchased by William Waldorf Astor.

Astor lavished his considerable fortune upon the estate, renovating the castle, building the "Tudor village", and creating the wonderful gardens. Hever is now in the hands of a private company.

The interior of Hever features some excellent Tudor furniture, portraits, and tapestries, as well as a costumed figure exhibit in the Long Gallery. There are exhibitions relating to Henry VIII and Anne, as well as a room devoted to a rather grisly display of medieval instruments of torture. Two illuminated Books of Hours inscribed by Anne Boleyn are proudly displayed.

The Gardens
The moated castle provides the historical backdrop for the formal gardens established by William Astor between 1904-1908. The gardens contain a wonderful variety of features, the most famous of which is the yew maze (open April - October weather

permitting). Of more horticultural significance is the Italianate Garden, designed to display Astor's collection of Italian sculpture.

The garden setting was enhanced by the creation of the lake, which stretches to 35 acres in size. It took two years of digging to create the lake, and as many as 800 men were involved in the digging at one time.

The most notable theme throughout the gardens is the use of water, with a multitude of water features, including fountains, ponds, a cascade, and, of course, the lake which I've already mentioned. Classical statuary is advantageously placed throughout.

Mention must be made of Anne Boleyn's Walk, lined by trees planted over 100 years ago, and the Splashing Water Maze, which has proved especially popular with children.

Also of interest to children of all ages is the Miniature Model Houses exhibit. Commissioned by the current owner of Hever, this collection of marvellous miniatures depicts life from Domesday England to the time of the Victorian country house - all in 1/12th scale!

Leeds Castle

Address: Maidstone, Kent, England, ME17 1PL

A former royal palace begun in the 12th century, Leeds Castle has to be one of the most beautifully situated medieval castles in England, projecting into its natural lake, and surrounded by 500 acres of beautiful parkland and gardens. Leeds has been owned by a succession of monarchs, and no less than six queens of England.

History
There was a Saxon royal manor here as early as 857 AD, After the Norman invasion, the manor was held by the Crevecoeur family (literal translation, "breakheart"), who rebuilt the manor as a stone dwelling. That early castle saw action during the turbulent conflict between King Stephen and Queen Maud, and in 1139 Stephen captured it from Maud's supporters.

From 1278 the castle belonged to the crown. In that year Edward I began building the barbican and the unusual fortified mill. Edward gave Leeds Castle as a dower gift to both his wives, Eleanor and Margaret, thus starting a tradition that frequently saw the castle owned by the queen of England.

Among queens who have owned Leeds Castle (apart from Eleanor and Margaret) are Isabella of France, Joan of Navarre,

Anne of Bohemia, and Catherine of Valois. Despite ostensible royal control, Isabella, queen to Edward II, was refused entry by the constable of the castle in 1321.

The king had to besiege the castle to wrest it from the constable's power. He also wrested the constable's head from his shoulders! From that point, Leeds seems to have gained a reputation as being a "ladies castle".

Leeds Castle was greatly enjoyed by Henry VIII, who added many of the Tudor windows. Henry stayed at Leeds on his way to his famous meeting with Francis I of France at the Field of the Cloth of Gold in 1520. Marvellous paintings in the Banqueting Hall portray the event.

After Henry's death, the castle was granted to a courtier by Edward VI, and it passed out of royal control forever. Over the years it saw service as a garrison, a convalescent home, a prison, and an opulent private home. Some of the most powerful families to own the property include the Wykham Martins, Culpeppers, and Fairfaxes.

In the 17th century, the castle was sold to Sir Anthony St. Leger, whose descendants built an estate house on the largest of the islands in Leeds lake. This house was later sold to the Culpeper family, who successfully managed to support both sides in the Civil War and the subsequent Restoration.

Finally, in the 20th century, the house passed to Olive Wilson Filmer, Lady Baillie, who spent considerable time and money refurbishing the interior and turning the living quarters into a sumptuous treasure trove stocked with ceramics, paintings, furniture, and tapestries.

Lady Baillie was a famous society hostess in the 1920s and 1930s, and many famous guests stayed at Leeds Castle during her tenure. It was Lady Baillie who established the Leeds Castle Foundation, which has administered the castle since her death.

The castle is set on a pair of small islands in a large lake. The lake is probably not natural, it was created sometime before 1272. The bulk of the buildings are still as they were laid out by Edward I, with later additions by Henry VIII, and a good deal of Victorian work to make the effect a bit prettier and less fortress-like!

The lake narrows to form a moat crossed by a drawbridge to an imposing gatehouse. Beside the bridge are the ruins of an unusual barbican with arches for the three roads that used to converge on this spot.

Within an outer bailey are two residential blocks, Maiden's Tower, built by Henry VIII, later used as a bakehouse, and a massive neo-Gothic block added by Fiennes Wykeham-Martin around 1820. This opulent block of rooms stands on the foundations of medieval apartments. Beyond this mansion, a passage leads to the smaller island. This passage replaces an earlier causeway and drawbridge.

On the smaller island is a D-shaped shell keep known as the Gloriette, built around a small courtyard. The lower parts of the keep were the work of Edward I, but the upper sections were rebuilt by Henry VIII. Though the interior contains some original timbers and panelling, it has been largely altered by subsequent generations to create a comfortable dwelling place.

The Gardens

The extensive parkland surrounding the castle was landscaped in the early 18th century. Many of the trees that were planted then still remain. The park is split by streams and lakes that are home to over 30 species of waterfowl. The Duckery provides habitat for ducks, geese, and swans. There is a lovely woodland garden, at its best in spring when daffodils, narcissi, and anemones are in bloom, and an English Cottage Garden. Leeds Castle is also home to the National Collection of Bergamot.

In the gardens is the yew Maze, planted and trimmed to resemble a topiary castle. Within the Maze is a secret underground grotto. The Leeds Castle vineyard was mentioned in the Domesday Book, and after a break of five centuries, the fruits of the vineyard are once again being used to produce fine wine.

Younger children especially will enjoy the maze, which exits through an underground grotto with appropriately eerie lighting effects. They will also enjoy the regular falconry exhibitions involving birds of prey from the aviary. There is a pay and play golf course, hot air balloon flights, a vineyard, dog collar museum, craft centre, and 'Go Ape', a high wire forest adventure area.

Leeds Castle is a very popular attraction, especially on sunny summer weekends, but it is well worth a visit at any time; the combination of a beautiful setting and a superlative historic treasure of a castle makes for an unforgettable day out.

The castle hosts a year-round schedule of special events, including open-air concerts, a vintage car gathering, firework display, and ballooning festival.

Rochester Castle

Address: The Keep, Rochester, Medway, Kent, England, ME1 1SW

One of the finest Norman keeps in England, Rochester Castle stands near the Cathedral, overlooking the River Medway. The castle was built on the site of an earlier Roman fort, and the keep uses building materials from the old Roman city walls.

History

The city of Rochester grew up around an important crossing of the River Medway, where the Roman Watling Street struck north towards London. Soon after the Norman Conquest, a timber fortification was built to guard the crossing, situated on Boley Hill, just south of the current castle site.

In 1088 Bishop Odo of Bayeux rebelled against William II, and garrisoned the castle with his Norman supporters. In a curious twist for a Norman lord, William drew up an army of native English soldiers. He besieged the castle and forced the garrison to surrender. His rebellion crushed, Odo fled into exile.

At this point, Gundulf, Bishop of Rochester, took a hand. Gundulf agreed to rebuild the castle in stone, at his own expense, if William would confirm Rochester Cathedral's rights of a manor. The king agreed, and Gundulf took over.

The bishop was a talented builder; he did not just hire a master mason, he actually oversaw the work himself. Gundulf moved the castle to a more secure site, partly protected by the Roman defences. He built a great curtain wall to surround his new stone fortress, but it was left to William de Corbeil, Archbishop of Canterbury, to build the massive stone keep that is the centrepiece of the castle we see today.

This is the largest keep in England, rising 113 feet from its base to the top of the four corner turrets. The keep is accessed through a huge forebuilding, which adds an extra set of defences for attackers to breach. The forebuilding originally gave access to the keep by a stair to the first-floor level and housed a chapel above a dungeon.

The Siege Of Rochester 1215
The Archbishops of Canterbury continued to act as constables of Rochester Castle until 1215 when the most powerful nobles in the realm rebelled against King John. Archbishop Stephen Langton handed the castle over to the rebellious barons, who garrisoned the fortress against the king. King John raised an army and attacked Rochester.

A concerted bombardment failed to breach the walls, so John ordered his sappers to dig a tunnel under the castle walls. This they did, and a section of the curtain wall collapsed. The rebels retreated into the central stone keep, so John ordered the mine extended. When the tunnel was completed the attackers used the fat from 40 pigs to fire the mine, causing a corner of the keep to collapse. Even then, the rebels did not surrender but retreated behind a cross-wall that divided the keep in two. They only surrendered when food and water ran out.

Henry III repaired the castle in the 1220s, but Rochester was again a focus for rebellion in 1264. Simon de Montfort led an army against the royal garrison and forced a breach in the curtain wall, but the defenders were saved when a royal army arrived and forced De Montfort's rebels to withdraw. The damage to the castle's defences was not restored until the reign of Edward III, who strengthened the walls against the threat of a French invasion.

The castle saw no further military action but remained a usable fortress until the 16th century. It passed into private ownership in the 17th century and was allowed to fall into disrepair. The corporation of Rochester bought the site in 1884 and turned the castle grounds into a public pleasure garden.

The 12th century keep built by Archbishop Corbeil remains essentially intact, just missing its floors and roof. It is 5 storeys high and includes a 'double storey' that houses a solar (private quarters for the lord) and the hall. The interior is divided by a cross-wall, at the base of which is a deep well.

The well-shaft rises the full height of the dividing wall so that defenders at every level could always have access to fresh water. The original three corner turrets are square, but the turret restored by Henry III after the siege of 1215 is circular, an indication of how military architecture had changed in the century since the original keep was built. Long sections of the curtain wall still stand, some of it still following the line of the old Roman city walls.

Note: Though listed as an English Heritage property, the castle is actually managed by Medway Council.

Scotney Castle

Address: Lamberhurst, Tunbridge Wells, Kent, England, TN3 8JN

In 1377 French ships raided the Sussex coast, causing widespread damage and panic among the local population. Roger de Ashburnham, Conservator of the Peace in Kent and Sussex, decided to build a castle to guard against the threat of further invasions.

He chose a site on the River Bewl, at the bottom of a wooded valley just south of Lamberhurst, and there he built a quadrangular castle on a pair of islands, surrounded by a wide moat. The moat also encloses an outer courtyard and the stumpy remains of a ruined gatehouse.

Only one of the original four towers still stands, topped with a later conical roof and bristling with machicolations. It looks for all the world like a fairytale castle tower, so much so that you almost expect to see a Disney fairy princess at the upper window of the tower.

It is possible that the quadrangular castle was never actually finished, and what we see today is a large part of the completed structure. The south tower we see today was recorded as the only tower standing in 1558.

The tower is connected to a later Elizabethan manor house, built by the Darrell family. Thomas Darrell owned the castle in the late

16th century, at a time when Catholicism was illegal. For seven years between 1591-1598 Darrell harboured a Catholic priest in a secret chamber inside the castle. You can see the secret chamber, hidden behind a cupboard door set into the stairwell.

On one occasion the priest, a Jesuit named Father Richard Blount, was forced to flee over a wall and across the moat to escape a raid by the authorities.

An east range was built by William Darrell around 1630, possibly to a design by Inigo Jones. Darrell had most of the medieval castle pulled down and connected his new house to the surviving tower. The manor followed the same route to decay as the medieval castle, and together they form the centrepiece of a magnificent hillside garden.

In 1778 Edward Hussey bought Scotney from the Darrell family. Around 1830 his grandson, also named Edward, called in architect Anthony Salvin to create a new Victorian mansion at the top of the hill, looking out across the valley towards the riverside ruins.

Salvin was one of the most popular society architects of his day and was known for designing houses in a mock-Elizabethan style. Not only did Salvin design the house, he also designed some of the furniture, for example the four-poster bed in the aptly named 'Salvin Bedroom'.

The picturesque view towards the medieval castle was accentuated by quarrying away part of the hillside for building stone. One unexpected treasure lurks in the quarry; the footprint of an iguanodon, left here over 100 million years ago.

Hussey planted a profusion of trees and masses of azaleas and rhododendrons, so that Scotney is a blaze of colour in early summer. His descendant, Christopher Hussey, left the estate to the National Trust, and the Trust has its regional headquarters here. Margaret Thatcher had an office in the mansion, and the house appeared in the 1979 film *Yanks*, starring Richard Gere.

In recent years the mansion house has been restored and opened to the public. There is a timed admission system to keep the numbers of visitors in the house at any one time down to a manageable level, but I highly recommend waiting for an available time slot; the mansion is a wonderful Victorian house, with richly panelled staterooms, and a mix of 'upstairs' and 'downstairs' rooms open to view. You really get a sense of what it was like to live and work in a large Victorian country house.

Look for the Hussey family coat of arms over the door with its Latin motto 'Vix ea nostra voco', which translates loosely as 'we scarcely call these things our own'.

From the Library, you get a wonderful view down the hill to the ruined castle and the picturesque garden that surrounds it. You can also see as far as the historic house of Finchcocks and to Goudhurst village.

Another unexpected delight is a series of watercolour paintings by Henrietta Windsor-Clive, the great-granddaughter of Clive of India. The paintings depict Henrietta's travels in Italy prior to her marriage to Edward Hussey III, who built the house.

The estate stretches to 770 acres, with trails through the hillside gardens and through lovely woodland. It truly is a gorgeous location; the garden is a delight, and the views across the wooded valley are superb.

Visiting Scotney Castle
Scotney is a gem; the views from the winding path down the hillside gardens prepare you for the Old Castle, but it is only when you walk around the moated site that it really hits you how pretty it is.

Some of that 'prettiness' is forced; it's a deliberate attempt by Edward Hussey to create a picturesque landscape, but in this case, it works so well that you don't mind if Hussey accentuated the ruined state of the medieval castle and Elizabethan manor for artistic effect. It works! I've seldom seen a more wonderfully romantic English castle.

Countryside attractions in Kent

Bewl Water

Address: Bewlbridge Lane, Lamberhurst, Kent, England, TN3 8JH

One of the finest recreational areas in the south of England, and the largest inland body of water in the south-east, Bewl Water is a man-made lake set in the midst of the Weald Area of Outstanding Natural Beauty. The lake is just the centrepiece of an 800-acre countryside park offering stunning scenery.

Surrounding the lake are 13 miles of walking trails, with family play areas. There are a variety of recreational opportunities, with sailing, fishing, and cycle hire. You can also take a pleasure cruise on the lake.

On the northern side of the reservoir is a family activity centre with an adventure playground and children's activities such as quad biking and model boating. The Bewl Water Outdoor Centre, operated by Kent County Council, offers adventure activity programmes for youth groups and schools, including rock climbing, orienteering, canoeing, and sailing.

The Bewl Water Walk is a 12.5-mile walking trail following the shore of the lake. The trail is open to walkers, horse riders, and cyclists (bring your own cycle or rent). On the southern side of the reservoir the trail borders a nature reserve.

History
By the middle of the 20th century, it was obvious that the Medway towns of Kent and Sussex needed a reliable source of water. The area's growing population meant that relying on the underground aquifer simply would not be sufficient.

The Bewl area had the advantage of being close to the target destination for water, yet relatively isolated and sparsely populated. In addition, there were local deposits of clay and sandstone which could be easily quarried and used to create a reservoir.

Work began in 1973. A 900m dam was built using clay quarried on-site, reinforced with local sandstone blocks. The bank was protected with a layer of gravel topped by concrete slabs to counter erosion. Pipes ran under the dam so that the River Bewl could continue to flow as it had always done.

Two concrete towers were added; one to act as an overflow and the other to draw off water. The lake created by the dam covers roughly 770 acres of land. Construction finished in 1975.

The Bewl reservoir holds over 31,000 million litres of water and provides drinking water for large areas of Sussex and Kent. There is enough water in the reservoir to provide an average of 150 litres of water to 200 million people every day.

Bewl Water is signposted off the A21 south of Lamberhurst. Next to the reservoir is a visitor centre with a restaurant and conference venue. Be aware that there is a charge for parking.

White Cliffs of Dover

Address: Langdon Cliffs, Upper Road, Dover, Kent, England, CT16 1HJ

The iconic White Cliffs are one of the most treasured British sites - and sights!

The iconic chalk cliffs of Dover are familiar to people across the globe and are one of the most easily recognised of England's natural landmarks. The cliffs and associated coastal landscape are home to an array of rare plants, birds, and animals; and has been declared a Site of Special Scientific Interest (SSSI). The area has also been named a Heritage Coast and an Area of Outstanding Natural Beauty (AONB).

A National Trust visitor centre offers displays explaining the natural history of the cliffs, while a network of footpaths run across the cliffs, providing for stunning coastal walks.

The White Cliffs were formed over the course of several million years from the accumulated remains of millions of small sea plants and animals. The porous nature of the chalk means that it is at continuous risk of erosion from the action of the water, and up to 5cm of cliffs are lost each year.

The cliff face offers roosting territory for a large and varied bird population, and inland of the cliffs is a lovely area of grassland and scrub offering further animal, insect, and bird habitat. It is hard to imagine today, but the clifftops were originally covered with trees. These were gradually cleared away by our ancestors to provide land for cultivation and grazing.

At one end of the White Cliffs is the South Foreland Lighthouse, a historic lighthouse that received the first ship to shore transmission in 1898, and transmitted the first cross-Channel wireless message in 1899. It was also the site of Faraday's first successful electric light. There are guided walks to the lighthouse from Spring to Autumn. There is a signposted walk to the lighthouse, which takes about 45-50 minutes, not counting time taken to stop and enjoy the fabulous views!

Guided tours of the White Cliffs are available from the National Trust visitor centre. There is also a wide network of public footpaths, offering self-guided and signposted trails. The long-distance Saxon Shore Way trail runs along the cliffs as well.

There are two signposted walks from the visitor centre. I mentioned the longer walk to the South Foreland Lighthouse. The other, shorter, walk is to Langdon Hole, a wide bay offering good views of the cliffs to the east. This walk takes about 20 minutes from the visitor centre. The area around Landon Bay is rich in naval archaeology, with several finds of ancient seagoing vessels found in the shallow waters at the base of the cliffs. An information panel explains the archaeological finds.

The White Cliffs are well signposted from all major roads around Dover, and there is plenty of parking in the National Trust car park. Most of the year the car park opens at dawn and closes at 7pm, so be aware of the time!

Historic Churches in Kent

By far the most popular historic church in the county is Canterbury Cathedral, a destination for pilgrims since the 12th century, but there are a wonderful variety of other fascinating churches to see. Look for the Heritage Rating to get an idea of how we ranked each church for its historic interest.

Barfreston, St Nicholas Church
Address: Barfreston, Kent, England

Superbly carved Norman south door, one of the finest in the country.

The small church of St Nicholas in Barfreston (or Barfrestone) is one of the hidden gems of Norman architecture in Kent, possibly in all of England. In the medieval period, the village of Barfreston was a stopover place for pilgrims on their way to the shrine of St Thomas a Becket at Canterbury. That may account for the likeness of Becket carved on the south door, the first known representation of Becket in the country.

Ah, the south door. Forgive me while I wax lyrical! If you enjoy Norman architecture. or just medieval architecture in general, you are in for a treat! The tympanum and arches of the south door boast some of the finest Norman carvings in Britain. At the centre of the tympanum is a figure of Christ. At his feet are two mermaids, a gryphon, and a figure of a sphinx.

Above this figure are three semi-circular bands of carvings. The first is simply a band of leaves. The second contains 12 medallions, featuring strange beasts playing musical instruments. One theory is that the masons were inspired by popular bestiaries of the day.

From left to right we see three figures playing instruments (a hare with a flageolet, an ape with pan pipes, and a woman with a dulcimer), a bear playing the harp, carousing beasts, a Miming figure, a hare toasting a partridge, a pair of lovers, two men arguing, a horse rider, a falconer, hounds chasing a hare, a churchman, and, finally, a monkey riding a goat, carrying a dead hare.

The third band of carvings draws on signs of the zodiac and the 'labours of the months'. Here we find two rams butting heads, a peacock, a pair of manticores (beasts with human heads), dragons, a gryphon, and a hedgehog.

The door has several scratch dials, a form of primitive sundial. The east wall of the church has a superb wheel window, with eight spokes radiating out from the centre. Beneath the wheel window are three deeply splayed lancet windows.

Around the eaves are a wonderful collection of carved heads, of the type normally (but erroneously) called gargoyles. These are both human and animal in form, and bear comparison with the justly famous carvings at Kilpeck, in Herefordshire. These carved heads may represent Christianised versions of earlier pagan tree gods and fertility symbols.

The church is small, stretching less than 50 feet from west to east. It was probably founded in the late 11th century by a Norman knight named Hugo de Port. That early Norman building was remodelled around 1180, with the addition of over 100 superb carvings that we can see today. It is possible that the 12th-century carvings were funded by Adam de Port, Hugo's great-grandson, as thanks for a beneficial marriage he contracted in 1180.

The north door, now blocked up, has some extremely interesting carvings of grotesque faces on the door jambs. Facing each other across the door opening are two faces, one grimacing as if in deep pain, another in an attitude of despair.

The interior of St Nicholas is fairly plain, with the exception of a monument to Thomas Boys. The chancel arch is quite beautifully carved, with traditional Norman saw tooth and zig-zag patterns. Beneath the windows of the nave is a beautifully carved string course, with human and animal figures.

Another unusual feature of St Nicholas church is that the bell does not hang in a belfry, but, rather, it is fixed in the branches of a tall yew tree outside the west end of the church, between the churchyard and the village pub next door, called, appropriately enough, the Yew Tree Inn.

All in all, the little church of St Nicholas at Barfreston is an absolute delight; one of the finest examples of Norman architecture in England, and well worth a visit.

Benenden, St George's Church

Address: Benenden, Kent, England

Kitty Fisher, of nursery rhyme fame, is buried in the Norris family vault

There was a church at Benenden at the time of the Domesday Book survey in 1086, making Benenden one of only four parishes in the Weald rich enough to have a church. That early building was enlarged in the 13th century when the current south porch was created.

Sometime around 1418, a huge detached bell tower was added. This was a remarkable structure of wood, on a stone foundation. The tower reached 132 feet in height, much higher than the current tower.

Also in the early 15th century, the north porch with its vaulting and carved gargoyles was added. The vaulting meets in a centrepiece representing a salamander; the symbol of eternal life in medieval Christian symbology. Each corner of the vaulting shafts terminates in a corbel head in the shape of peculiar faces or masks.

The bell tower was unfortunately struck by lightning in 1672. The tower was burned to the ground, and all five bells melted from the extreme heat. The tower was not replaced until 1718, with money earned from investing the proceeds of selling the scrap metal from the old bells. When the church was rebuilt, it was with a sturdy, integrated tower.

Benenden church was heavily rebuilt in 1861 by architect David Brandon, under the direction of Rt Hon. Gawthorne-Hardy, later first Earl of Cranbrook. Memorials to the Gawthorne-Hardy family can be seen in the chancel.

Also within the church is a memorial to Sir John Norris, Lord of the Admiralty, who owned the manor of Hemsted House. Norris's grandson, also named John, married Kitty Fisher, a famous courtesan who is remembered in a popular nursery rhyme. Fisher is buried in the Norris family vault under the chancel.

There is also a memorial brass to Edmund Gibbon, who founded the local school in 1609.

In the churchyard is the grave of an early cricketer by the name of Richard Mills, whose gravestone is carved with a cricket bat.

Brabourne, Kent, St Mary's Church

Address: The Street, Brabourne, Kent, England, TN25 5LR

Our first written record of a church Brabourne comes from 1070, shortly after Lanfranc became Archbishop of Canterbury. That first church was replaced by the Norman building we can see today in 1144. The most immediately obvious external feature is the very squat and sturdy west tower, heavily braced with buttresses rising in seven stages on the diagonal and five stages in the centre of the south tower wall.

The original tower was much higher, but around 1700 it began to collapse, so the upper stages were taken down and the buttresses added to prevent a total collapse. The tower stair is built of oak timbers, 31 feet long, with a forked branch to support it and another oak timber as the base. Each tread is triangular, fixed by an oak peg.

Set on the nave walls are a pair of lead panels inscribed with the initials TW and TT, for Thomas Thompson and Thomas Webb, churchwardens in 1700, commemorated for their role in rebuilding the medieval tower. Also in the nave is a coat of arms to George II, over the south door.

The Chancel
The east end of St Mary's is a delight. The chancel arch is 12th century, with carved capitals and string-courses. On the south

side are a carved dragon and a human head with long hair. The easternmost arch of the south wall is decorated with laughing faces of monks.

Set into the north wall of the chancel is an elaborately carved 15th-century tomb of John Scott (d. 1485), Lord Warden of the Cinque Ports and Comptroller of the Household to Edward IV. The tomb recess is set beneath a beautifully decorated canopy and has a lower section showing the arms of Scott and Beaufitz.

It seems likely that the tomb once had an effigy of Sir John or memorial brasses, but if so, they are gone now. The altar, topped with Bethersden marble, dates to about 1600 and was originally a table tomb for Reginald Scott (d. 1599), author of Discovery of Witchcraft, a popular treatise on the matter of witches. The altar is inscribed with versions of the Scott family arms, the earliest from 1290 and the last from 1562.

On opposite sides of the chancel walls are mounted helmets of Sir William Scott (d. 1433, south wall) and Sir Thomas Scott (d. 1594, north wall). Sir Thomas has a place in British legend, having raised 4,000 men in 24 hours when the Spanish Armada neared the coast of Kent in 1585. Two arched niches on the south wall originally contained more Scott tombs, one probably that of Sir

William Scott, Lord Chief Justice and Knight Marshall of England, who died in 1350.

The Norman Window
High in the north wall of the chancel, above the altar, is a small, deeply splayed Norman window. At first glance it is unremarkable; a typical example of a round-headed Norman window. But set within the window is stained glass from about the year 1200, and what is even more remarkable is that the glass is in exactly the same place in which it was placed over 800 years ago.

This makes the Brabourne window the oldest in the country with its original glass intact, in its original setting, or as the church guide rather colourfully puts it, "It is believed that this is the oldest complete Norman window through which light falls anywhere in England".

By contrast, the lovely east window is filled with stained glass by the Ward and Hughes company and won first prize at the prestigious Paris Exhibition of 1878.

The Balliol Heart Shrine
One feature above all others sets Brabourne church apart, and it can be found immediately beside the arch leading to the Scott

chapel from the chancel. This is a small, richly decorated niche, topped by a slab of Bethersden marble and carved with a cross within a circle.

At the back of the shrine is a recess, called a *'feretum'*, where an embalmed heart would have been set, encased in silver or ivory. This 'heart shrine' thought to have once contained the embalmed heart of John Balliol, father of John Balliol 'le Scot' who briefly became king of Scotland.

The elder Balliol founded Balliol College at Oxford University, and after his death, his grieving wife bore his heart around her neck in a casket of ivory and silver, day and night.

The heart was buried with her at Sweetheart Abbey, near Dumfries, but after the younger Balliol was defeated by Edward I the abbey was despoiled. Balliol, whose descendants bore the name of Scott, resided for a time at Brabourne before his eventual exile by Edward.

He was by conviction a Cluniac, and since Brabourne was at that time held by the Cluniac monks of Monks Horton, it seems logical that he brought his father's embalmed heart to Brabourne and set in within the shrine.

The heart shrine is empty now, and no one knows what became of the heart. Perhaps it was lost in the Reformation, but we don't really know, and that just adds to the intrigue.

The Scott Chapel

Originally known as the Holy Trinity Chapel, the Scott Chapel dates to 1420 and is full to bursting with memorials to members of the Scott family. The earliest memorial, however, predates the chapel. It is a small 13th-century coffin lid set into the centre of the chapel floor, between an array of Scott family brasses.

Some of the brasses have been strikingly reset in black marble, among them is one to Sir William Scott, who founded the chapel and served as sword-bearer to Henry V, and a later Sir William Scott who was Constable of Dover Castle, Lord Warden of the Cinque Ports, and attended Henry VIII at the Field of the Cloth of Gold.

On the north side of the chapel is a brass to Isabel, Lady Clifton, wife of the first Sir William. This brass is unusual in that Lady Clifton is shown without a head-dress. Another brass shows Elizabeth Powynynges, the daughter of Sir John Scott, whose tomb niche is in the chancel.

There is also a rather sad memorial is to Francis Talbot Scott, who died of melancholy (depression) after he was forced to sell off the family estates.

Brook, Kent, St Mary's Church

Address: The Street, Brook, Kent, England, TN25 5PF

The small rural village of Brook is accessed via narrow, winding lanes, and the setting of the ancient church of St Mary in its leafy churchyard is an idyllic one, in perfect keeping with its peaceful surroundings. St Mary's is one of the most complete Norman churches in England, dating almost entirely to the late 11th century.

Rather than being an independent parish church, St Mary's was owned from the start by Canterbury Cathedral, which perhaps explains how it has remained so unaltered by the passage of time.

The interior architecture is simple, even rough. But that simple interior was embellished in the 13th century by a series of wall paintings which rank among the finest in England. Though the worn nave paintings are interesting, especially a large figure of St

Christopher over the north door, it is in the chancel that Brook shines.

Most of the east wall, and large sections of the north and south chancel walls are covered with a pattern of roundels painted with Biblical scenes. The east wall paintings are in a striking monochrome scheme, alternately black on white and white on black.

The major themes are the Resurrection, Nativity, and the Passion. On the south wall are red on white and white on red depictions of scenes from the life of a saint.

There is a further painting of Christ in Majesty in the tower, in what was once a private chapel. This is the earliest painting in the church, dating to the 12th century, but it can only be viewed by previous appointment, as the tower is normally kept locked.

There are 14th-century floor tiles in the chancel floor, in front of the stone altar slab. The altar was buried in the churchyard during the Reformation and only discovered again in 1966. Beside the altar stone are a 14th-century piscina and single-seat sedilia of the same period.

The most striking feature of the church exterior is the sturdy west tower. This rises in three stages, the second of which has traditionally ben known as the 'Priest's Room', used as accommodation for priests from Canterbury coming to administer the manor of Brook. The west tower door has reused pieces of a Norman frieze set into the tympanum.

One other unusual feature is worth mentioning; in the north wall of the chancel is a small almond-shaped opening, protected by deep splays. This is probably the remains of a medieval squint, or hagioscope, allowing an anchorite to view the high altar.

There are no apparent traces of an anchorite cell attached to the chancel, so we can only presume it was destroyed during the Reformation.

I found Brook church a delight to visit. The combination of the setting, the beautifully complete Norman building, and the wonderful wall paintings make it a memorable place to see.

Burham, St Mary's Church

Address: Church Road, Burham, Kent, England, ME1 3XY

St Mary's is a historic church beside the River Medway, on the ancient pilgrim's route to Canterbury. The church is built of local ragstone and flint and consists of a nave, chancel, a west tower. An octagonal stair turret climbs the south-west angle of the tower. There used to be north and south aisles, but these were pulled down at some point in the past.

St Mary's stands opposite Snodland church on the far bank of the Medway. The towers of the two churches are very similar, suggesting that they were both used as shelters by pilgrims crossing the river here.

In the 19th century, the entire village of Burham moved to higher ground, and built a new church, leaving St Mary's in isolated splendour. Ironically, the newer church has itself been pulled down.

St Mary's has features from every time period, leading it to be dubbed 'an Alphabet of English Church Architecture'. The oldest part of this particular alphabet is a collection of Roman tiles taken from local Romano-British villas.

Aside from the Roman tiles, the oldest part of the building is Norman. The main structure of the building is 12th century, with 13th-century nave arcades, and there are two Norman fonts, one decorated with traditional Romanesque carving.

The west tower rises in four stages to a crenellated top and dates to the 14th century. It may have been paid for by offerings from pilgrims.

The church was unfortunately in the news for all the wrong reasons in 2013 after thieves broke in and stole a tall brass crucifix and a pair of candles.

The church is no longer used for regular worship and is in the care of the Churches Conservation Trust.

Canterbury Cathedral

Address: Canterbury, Kent, England, CT1 2EH

Even if Thomas Becket had chosen somewhere else to earn his martyr's crown, Canterbury would still deserve attention for its role in the spread of Christianity throughout England. It was here that St. Augustine began the conversion of the pagan islanders in 597.

History
St Augustine built a cathedral church within the old Roman city walls of Canterbury, and he became the first Archbishop of Canterbury. A Christian community grew up around the cathedral, managing the building and its environs. In the 10th

century this community formally became a Benedictine monastery.

The remains of the original 6th century cathedral established by Augustine lie beneath the nave. Excavation has shown that Augustine's church was built in part on top of a Roman road, presumably to provide a solid foundation.

Little enough remains of the Saxon church, for after the Norman conquest Archbishop Lanfranc rebuilt the cathedral on a more lavish scale. This rebuilding took seven years, from 1070 to 1077. The best surviving parts of this first Norman church are a staircase and the area of the north west transept known as The Martyrdom.

In 1170 Becket met his death in the north transept of the crossing (The Martyrdom) at the hands of four knights seeking to curry favour with Henry II, who had quarrelled with the Archbishop. Immediately after Becket's death miracles began to be reported at his tomb, and when the church suffered a major fire in 1172 it provided an excuse for rebuilding and making the cathedral a fitting shrine for the recent martyr.

The rebuilding was entrusted to William of Sens, who brought with him a mastery of the new French style, which we now call

"Gothic". In 1179 William of Sens fell from scaffolding above the high altar and was so badly injured that he was forced to retire and leave the project in the capable hands of his assistant, a man known to us only as William the Englishman.

Becket's shrine in the Trinity Chapel was finished in 1220, and for another 300 years it was the most popular place of pilgrimage in England (see Chaucer's Canterbury Tales). The Corona was built at the eastern end of the quire as a separate chapel to house a piece of Becket's skull.

In the 14th century Archbishop Lanfranc's nave was rebuilt by Henry Yevele, called the greatest architect of late medieval England. Yevele (or Yeveley) pushed the nave to the height of the chancel, creating a vast, upward-reaching hall. In 1496 the "Bell Harry" central tower was added. This is the tall tower that can be seen from many miles away.

Henry VIII's men despoiled Becket's tomb during the Dissolution of the Monasteries, carting away 26 wagon loads of valuables and scattering the bones of the saint.

The area where Becket's shrine stood is marked with a candle at the east end of the chancel. Before the candle is a pinkish stone set into the floor, which bears the marks of thousands of pilgrims who knelt there to worship at Becket's shrine. The impact of the sheer number of medieval pilgrims on the cathedral cannot be overstated; the staircase leading up to the south ambulatory - known as Trinity Stair - is worn into undulating waves by the passage of their feet and knees.

Canterbury, St Dunstan

Address: 80 London Road, Canterbury, Kent, England, CT2 8LS

A small church with historical associations to kings, martyrs, archbishops, and chancellors. The king in question was Henry II. After his conflict with Archbishop Thomas a Becket led to the latter's murder in Canterbury Cathedral, Henry performed a public penance. On 18 July 1174 he rode to the outskirts of Canterbury, where he stopped at St Dunstan's church, donned penitential garments, and removed his shoes. From here he walked barefoot to Becket's cathedral where he was scourged by the monks.

Three and a half centuries later and St Dunstan's once more played a part in the nation's history. Thomas More, then one of the most powerful men in the realm, was executed in 1535 for his refusal to bow to Henry VIII's claim to be head of the church in England.

After More's death, his head was brought here by Margaret Roper, his daughter. There is a head, of approximately the correct age, in the Roper family vault beneath St Nicholas Chapel. Is it Thomas More's? We don't know for sure, but it seems quite possible. In 1935 More was canonized, and St Nicholas's chapel became a place of pilgrimage.

The church itself was founded by Lanfranc, Archbishop of Canterbury, at the end of the 11th century. It was certainly the first in England to be dedicated to St Dunstan.

You enter St Dunstans by way of the 17th century south porch. Nearby is the vestry, initially a chapel founded in 1330 by Henry de Canterbury, chaplain to Edward III. Also at the west end is the font, a plain design that probably dates to the early medieval period. It is surmounted by an elaborate 15th-century wooden cover. Beside the font is an attractive ancient wooden chest for storing parish documents and other valuables.

The bells are worth noting; there are six of these, and the fifth dates to the 14th century. The nave and chancel exhibit details from the Early English, Decorated, and Perpendicular phases of Gothic.

St Nicholas Chapel (The Roper Chapel) is the highlight of any visit to St Dunstan's. It was created in 1402 as a chantry for 'John Roper, his parents, friends, and benefactors'. It is unusual in that it uses brick for a late Gothic structure, unlike the more common stone. The Roper family vault is beneath the chapel floor, and it is here that the head of St Thomas More is stored. Up above ground is the altar table, a fine Elizabethan piece of furniture.

A few hundred yards down St Dunstans Street is the Roper Gate, a Tudor gateway that is all that remains of Place House, home of William Roper and his wife Margaret, daughter of St Thomas More.

Canterbury, St Martin

Address: North Holmes Road, Canterbury, Kent, England, CT1 1QJ

St Martin's can claim to be the oldest church in England; certainly, it is the oldest still in regular use. St Augustine set up a church here when he arrived in Kent in AD 597 to convert the inhabitants to Christianity.

St Martins thus forms part of the Canterbury World Heritage Site, along with Canterbury Cathedral and St Augustine's Abbey. Unlike those other two historic attractions, St Martin's remains unknown to most visitors to Canterbury, and that's a real shame, for it is a lovely historic building.

It seems highly probable that St Martins predates the arrival of St Augustine in AD 597. At that time Kent was ruled by King AEthelbert, who had married a Frankish princess named Bertha. Bertha was already Christian, and when she came to Kent she brought her private chaplain. She worshipped in an existing Roman [Christian] church. From the description of that Roman church, it seems likely that it was the building that is now St Martins.

The oldest parts of St Martins are certainly built of Roman brick, but whether these are part of an early Roman structure, or simply reused by Bertha, or Augustine and his successors, we do not know for sure.

Parts of the chancel are almost certainly Roman, but the style of some brickwork may be 7th century. A blocked doorway in the south wall of the chancel is 7th-century work, as is round-headed doorway nearby. Is the chancel Roman, or does it simply reuse old Roman bricks?

The nave is buttressed in a way that suggests early Saxon work, and there are blocked windows in the west wall of the nave that are certainly Saxon. A relative newcomer amid all this ancient building is the chancel arch, which is Perpendicular Gothic.

The font is an absolute delight; it is a huge Norman tub, decorated with wonderfully intricate carvings of interlocking circles and arcading. It is built of Caen stone, highly prized by medieval builders.

There are several excellent brasses, and in the west tower is a huge memorial tablet to Sir John Finch (d. 1660). Finch is famous as the Speaker of the House of Commons who had to be held down in his chair to enable Parliament to pass the Petition of Right in 1628, limiting royal power.

St Martins is regularly open to visitors, and it is well worth a stroll from the historic core of Canterbury to see this historic old church.

Canterbury, St Mary Magdalene

Address: Burgate, Canterbury, Kent, England

The tower is all that remains of the medieval church of St Mary Magdalene. The church was pulled down in 1871 after it had become ruinous. The tower is a 1503 rebuilding of an earlier medieval structure.

In a specially built display area at the base of the tower is a fanciful Baroque memorial to the Whitfield family, dated 1680. This monument is in the Flemish style often associated with Grinling Gibbons and Arnold Quellin. It has been restored with the help of the Victoria and Albert Museum in London.

Beside the tower, in the area formerly occupied by part of the old church, is a pleasant garden area, behind which is the new(ish) Catholic church of St. Thomas of Canterbury.

One of the bells of St Mary Magdalene was transferred to St George the Martyr church, which itself was pulled down after it suffered bomb damage in WWII.

Canterbury, St Mildred Church

This ancient church is the oldest pre-Conquest church still standing within the city walls of Canterbury. It is a few short steps away from the remains of Canterbury Castle.

St Mildred's dates back to the Saxon period. It was badly damaged by a fire in 1246, with the result that much of the current building is of 13th-century construction. Much earlier though are the large quoins of the south-west corner of the church; these are reused Roman stones. The majority of the windows are 14th century, while the north aisle was added in 1486.

One of the most interesting features of the interior is the king-post roof construction. This is 14th-century work, and utilizes huge timbers.

Another interesting feature is the font. This is fairly plain and dates to 1420. What makes it interesting, though, is that it retains its original cover and lifting mechanism for raising that cover. The carved bench ends date from 1520 and were brought from St John's church when that building was demolished.

The south-east chapel was built in 1512 by Thomas Attwood, four times Mayor of Canterbury. Unusually, a small fireplace is set into the wall of the chapel. Just above and to the left of the fireplace is a window containing a small section of 13th century stained glass depicting St Mildred.

Near the pulpit is a monument to Sir Thomas Cranmer (d. 1640). Cranmer was the nephew of Archbishop Thomas Cranmer, he of Reformation fame.

In the churchyard, behind the east end of the church, is the grave of Alderman Simmons, who donated Dane John Gardens to the city of Canterbury.

Address: Church Lane, Canterbury, Kent, England, CT1 2PP

Family Attractions in Kent

Bredgar & Wormshill Light Railway

Address: The Warren, Bredgar, Kent, England, ME9 8AT

The B&W is a historic narrow-gauge railway in beautiful woodland in the heart of the Kentish Downs. See restored narrow gauge locomotives, beam engines, vintage vehicles and equipment, and a Dutch street organ.

Aside from steam rail equipment, the Bredgar and Wormshill railway has a number of steam-driven engines on view, including steam traction engines and farm equipment.

There is a collection of petrol-driven Bean vehicles, including a 1920s bus. You can see a replica Victorian steam-powered beam engine and pumping station.

Regular steam journeys go from Warren Wood Station in Bredgar to Stony Shaw Station at Wormshill.

Canterbury Historic River Tours

Address: Old Weavers House, 3 St Peter's St, Canterbury, Kent, England, CT1 2AT

One of the best ways to explore historic Canterbury is by river. Canterbury Historic River Tours provide regular tours from April to October along the river in flat-bottomed punts, departing from the Old Weavers House on St Peter's Street. Tours last approximately 45 minutes and take in some of Canterbury's most historic sights.

The very first of these sights is located immediately beside the departure dock; this is the old medieval ducking stool used to punish scolds or detect witches. The Old Weavers House itself is a lovely half-timbered historic building that may date to the 13th century.

Further along the river, you pass the island where Greyfriars priory was built in the 13th century. You will also see the last remaining parts of Blackfriars monastery, 12th-century Eastbridge Hospital, 12th century King's Bridge, and more historic locations on either side of the river.

The tours guides are also your boat pilot, and they provide an entertaining commentary and are willing to answer any questions you might have about the history of Canterbury or any of the sights you pass along the way.

Tours leave every 15-20 minutes and booking is not generally required. I very much enjoyed my excursion with Canterbury Historic River Tours and would definitely recommend it as a good way to get the most of a visit to Canterbury.

Chislehurst Caves

Address: Caveside Close, Old Hill, Chislehurst, Kent, England, BR7 5NL

An astonishing maze of underground tunnels and caverns runs deep under Chislehurst, created by the mining efforts of ancient inhabitants over the course of 8,000 years.

The first mines at Chislehurst were begun around 6000 BCE as our ancestors dug for flint to use in making tools. Those ancient mines were extended in the Roman and Saxon periods to produce a labyrinthine tangle composed of over 20 miles of passages.

Later miners searched the chalk soil for deposits of lime for use in plaster and whitewash. The mines were last worked in the 1830s, but by the late 19th century the caverns and tunnels at Chislehurst had become a popular tourist attraction for Victorian visitors.

In WWI the mines were used as an ammunition depot, an outpost of the Woolwich Arsenal. A narrow-gauge railway was established to speed up the movement of goods through the tunnels.

During WWII the mines were used as a large air-raid shelter; in fact, Chislehurst was the largest shelter outside London. Guided tours take visitors through the three main sections of the caves, separated into 'Druid', Saxon, and Roman areas.

Kent and East Sussex Railway

Address: Tenterden Town Station, Station Road, Tenterden, Kent, England, TN30 6HE

The Kent and East Sussex Railway is a historic light railway that runs for ten miles across the Kentish Weald, from the old market town of Tenterden to the historic 13th-century fortress of Bodiam Castle. For part of its route, the railway follows the course of the River Rother through attractive countryside.

There are stations at Tenterden, Northiam, and Bodiam, however there are no parking facilities at Bodiam Station, so visitors are advised to begin their journeys at either Northiam or Tenterden. The route also passes through Rolvenden and Wittersham Road Station on its way from Tenterden to Bodiam.

The Kent and East Sussex Railway opened in 1900 when it was known as the Rother Valley Railway. It was a light railway, intended to operate only until operating profits could be generated to rebuild it using more permanent heavy rail techniques.

In 1923 the railway introduced a unique carriage; a pair of Ford busses linked back to back and fitted with rail wheels. The railway could not compete with the convenience of road travel and finally ceased operation in 1954. A charitable society was formed with the aim of restoring the railway to passenger service, and regular service began again in 1974.

The railway uses a mix of steam and diesel locomotives, including two 'Terrier' steam locomotives built in 1872.

The K&ES railway also has special days out with 'guest' locomotives like Thomas the Tank Engine and his friends.

Romney, Hythe & Dymchurch Railway

Address: New Romney, Kent, England, TN28 8PL

One of the most famous light railways in Britain, the Romney, Hythe & Dymchurch Railway runs 14 miles across Romney Marsh from Hythe to Dungeness. The Dungeness terminus is directly beside the historic Old Lighthouse, a Grade-I listed building on Dungeness shingle beach.

At New Romney there is a miniature version of the mainline system and a Model Railway Exhibition. See historic engines and carriages being maintained, both steam and petrol-driven versions.

The railway opened to the public in 1927, when it was advertised as the smallest public railway in the world. The railway was created by JEP Howey and Count Louis Zborowski, owner of the real Chitty Chitty Bang Bang Mercedes racing car. They had special purpose-built engines built to haul carriages on a route from Hythe and New Romney.

The route was later extended to Dungeness. So popular was the railway that it soon had to use nine locomotives to handle all the visitors. The line was used by the military during WWII when it featured the only miniature armoured train in the world.

Following the war, the railway scaled back to its original two locomotives, but the regular journeys across Romney Marsh continue today, allowing visitors to experience this wonderfully scenic area in an unforgettable way. The trip takes in seven stations; Hythe, Dymchurch, St Mary's Bay, Romney Warren Halt, New Romney, Romney Sands, and Dungeness.

We visited the New Romney Station and explored the model railway exhibits. A few days later we were visiting the Old Lighthouse at Dungeness. By sheer chance, our visit coincided with the departure of a steam locomotive and we were able to watch the engine being loaded with water and coal, and build up a head of steam before heading out on a journey.

It is an amazing sight to see the old steam locomotives in action and see the billowing smoke and steam as they gather speed. The RH&DR is a delight, and is deservedly one of the most popular visitor attractions in Kent year after year. Trains run throughout the year, including special holiday service at Christmas time. Please refer to the official website for full timetables.

Note that even if you don't take a train trip you can still get a platform pass at New Romney, which allows you to explore the trains in the station and see the model railway exhibit. And if you are lucky like us you will see a train come steaming into the station while you are on the platform.

Spa Valley Railway

Address: West Station, Royal Tunbridge Wells, Kent, England, TN2 5QY

The Spa Valley Railway is a fascinating historic rail line on the border of East Sussex and Kent, running for 3.5 miles from Royal Tunbridge Wells to Groombridge. The main station is at the Old West Station in Tunbridge Wells (please note that there is no parking at the Groombridge end of the line).

The station is located in a former engine shed at the old station. Here you will find a collection of locomotives and rolling stock, as well as a restoration workshop where you can watch historic engines and carriages being restored.

The train service stops at High Rocks, an ancient geological area of sandstone cliffs. The end of the line is at Groombridge, where passengers can alight to visit 17th-century Groombridge Place historic house, and gardens. A joint ticket covering Groombridge Place and the rail journey is available.

There are a number of special runs throughout the year, including a Santa Special, and a day out with Thomas the Tank Engine and his friends. Rail service is a mix of steam and diesel locomotives. There are no less than 12 steam engines, 10 diesel engines, and a variety of 'visiting' engines. Among the carriages are several formerly used by the London Underground.

Tunbridge Wells West Station was opened in 1866 by the London Brighton & South Coast Railway in direct competition to an earlier station at Tunbridge Wells Central (now the main rail station for the town). The station had rail links to London and the south coast at Brighton and Eastbourne. Due to decreased use, the line from Eridge to Tunbridge Wells closed in 1985.

The line was purchased by a preservation group named the Tunbridge Wells and Eridge Railway Preservation Society. This group merged with the North Downs Steam Railway to form the Spa Valley Railway. The combined efforts of many volunteers resulted in the reopening of the line to Groombridge in 1998. As of this writing, plans are underway to open the line as far as Eridge.

Gardens in Kent

Bedgebury National Pinetum

Address: Park Lane, Goudhurst, Cranbrook, Kent, England, TN17 2SJ

One of the most extensive and varied collections of conifers in the world grace Bedgebury Pinetum. Much attention has been paid to creating gardens with colour and varieties of plants to provide interest at every season of the year.

History

In 1the 1850s Viscount William Beresford began to plant a pinetum surrounding the Park House, a lodge in his Bedgebury estate. The estate itself dates to at least the 9th century and was once visited by Elizabeth I. Beresford's stepson developed Lady

Mildred's Drive to enable visitors to the estate to comfortably view the pinetum from the comfort of their carriages.

In 1924 the Royal Botanic Gardens at Kew realised that growing air pollution in central London made caring for the National Conifer Collection increasingly difficult. They looked around for a suitable place for the conifer collection and settled on the Bedgebury estate because it already had the existing 19th-century pinetum in place.

The first new trees were planted at Bedgebury in 1925, centred on the valley around Marshall's Lake. From 1969 the pinetum has been managed by the Forestry Commission.

The Pinetum has over 10,000 conifers and other species, acting as a gene bank and genetic plant resource. There are over 2300 conifer species, including the tallest tree in Kent, an Abies grandis. The Pinetum holds 5 national collections, including thuja, Lawson's Cypress, juniper, yew, and Leyland Cypress. It also is home to more than 50 species that have been declared endangered.

The Bedgebury Pinetum is arguably the finest collection of conifers anywhere in the world and is set in a beautiful wooded valley with lakes and streams, gently rolling hills, and wide avenues giving visitors wonderful views.

There are nature trails through the woodland, as well as an adventure play area and cycling trails.

The Pinetum is open daily except at Christmas and during extreme weather conditions. There is an admission fee.

Chartwell

Chartwell was the family home of Winston Churchill; set in wonderful gardens with views across a private lake. An unremarkable exterior hides a comfortable family home, full of Churchill memorabilia, from cigars to paintings to war correspondence.

Winston Churchill purchased Chartwell in 1922 as a country retreat from the pressures of political life in London. He needed the escape, for his political career was at a low point in the early 1920s. He couldn't afford it, but he fell in love with the property and the wonderful view across the rolling hills of the Kentish Weald.

He went ahead with the purchase without consulting his wife Clementine, which predictably caused some marital friction.

Churchill called in architect Philip Tilden to transform what was essentially a villa into a cosy family home, designed to make the most of the wonderful views and the sloping site.

The centrepiece of the house is Churchill's study, where he wrote many of his works, particularly the historical books he produced after retiring from politics. He would often sleep in this room, and work either standing at a desk or pacing the floor, dictating to secretaries who were always on call.

Much of the remainder of Chartwell is less a house than a museum, crammed with memorabilia, from war uniforms to gifts given by political allies. Churchill's own paintings line the walls, softening the effect of glass display cases and information boards.

Visiting Chartwell
Visits to the house are by timed admission, but you are free to wander. If you can possibly avoid summer weekends I suggest you do so; we came on a sunny August day and it was extremely crowded. This wasn't a problem in the gardens and grounds but the house was very crowded and it was a bit difficult to easily enjoy all the rooms.

For Chartwell is not a stately home, with grand, spacious staterooms or showpiece halls; it is a comfortable house; a family home, and it was never made to handle the numbers of curious visitors who pass through the doors. If you do come at a busy time of year, I suggest you come early in the day!

Chartwell is set in a wonderful mix of formal and informal gardens dotted with little surprises like a tiny waterfall and a bench carefully placed to catch the eye. By the lakeshore is an oversized statue by Oscar Nemon of an elderly Churchill and his wife sitting side by side, while over the hedge you can make out the tip of a Kentish oast house.

Nemon was a firm friend of the Churchills and also crafted the famous statue of Sir Winston in the Members Lobby of the House of Commons in London.

A short distance from the house is the Studio, where Churchill retreated to follow his passion for painting. The Studio has slightly different opening times than the house itself, so please check the National Trust website if you'd like to enjoy a look at Churchill's private painting space and view his art on display.

Summing Up

Our family loved Chartwell. Though we visited on a Bank Holiday, when the summer sun shone brightly, and the house was full to bursting with fellow visitors, we found the experience of exploring the house and grounds an absolute delight. Yes, it was crowded. But, oh, what a wonderful experience. If you aren't particularly enamoured of Churchill, you will be after visiting, and if you already are, well, you'll need no second invitation!

Dane John Gardens

Address: Watling Street, Canterbury, Kent, England, CT1 2TN

Canterbury's largest and most popular garden. The intriguing name comes from an English mangling of the Norman French 'donjon' (forerunner of our word 'dungeon'). In this case, the term does not refer to a prison, but to an early Norman castle founded by William the Conqueror.

Shortly after the Conquest, William established castles at Canterbury, Dover, and Rochester. These were simple wooden structures atop a high mound, or motte. The high castle mound, known locally as Dane John's Mound, gives its name to the garden. However, the mound itself was in existence well before the Norman Conquest; it dates to at least the 1st century AD.

The park containing the garden was in place by 1551, but the formal gardens that stretch out at the foot of the mound were laid out around 1790 as a gift to the city by Alderman James Simmons. A memorial obelisk to Simmons stands at the top of Dane John Mound.

Simmons, whose grave can be seen at St Mildred's church, created a garden bounded on one side by an avenue of plane trees and on the other side by the old city walls. There is a play area, fountain, and bandstand where open-air events are held. Visitors and residents alike enjoy walks along the city walls, which give great views across the city.

Doddington Place Gardens

Address: Doddington, Sittingbourne, Kent, England, ME9 0BB

Ten acres of lovely landscape gardens surround a 19th-century manor. Here you will find woodland walks, rows of softly curving yew hedges, and an Edwardian rock garden, all in an attractive, informal setting.

History
In 1870 Sir John Croft asked architect Charles Trollope to design a mansion at Doddington. Three years later Croft called in

Markham Nesfield to lay out formal terraced garden beside his new house. Much of the Victorian gardens were altered in the Edwardian period, when General and Mrs Douglas Jeffreys added a mile of box hedging and a rock garden. Mrs Jeffreys used Kentish rag stone from a quarry at Maidstone to create a series of descending waterways that empty into a large pool.

What To See

The garden features a large area of woodland, where azaleas and rhododendron flourish. The Edwardian rock garden is dotted with small pools, and there is a sunken garden area with lush herbaceous borders.

One of the most picturesque features is a long grass walk terminating in a folly of brick and flint. Sir Roy Strong has called this folly 'a piece of Hampton Court', and it is easy to see why, for it resembles the Tudor palace in style and materials. Yet it is one of the most recent additions to the garden, designed in 1997 by Richard Oldfield as a memorial to his first wife.

Long yew hedges are still a feature at Doddington, and there are numerous old trees arranged around the estate. The hedges have grown and taken on striking amorphous shapes reminiscent of soft, puffy clouds.

The large pool installed in the Edwardian period has been remodelled so that one side looks like a quarry wall with water trickling down it. There is also a modern viewing platform over the pool. Around the rock garden are clustered a variety of shrubs, grasses, trees, and alpine plants.

Colours are at their best in May and June when the woodland garden is in full bloom. One feature of the woodland is a Wellingtonia Walk, laid out in the late Victorian period by Sir John Croft. The sunken garden flows from tulips early in the year to alliums, roses, and euphorbias later in the summer.

Doddington has featured in numerous magazine articles and acted as a setting for several films and TV series. The gardens are regularly open for the National Garden Scheme and on specified days from April-October.

Emmetts Garden

Address: Ide Hill, Sevenoaks, Kent, England, TN14 6BA

Emmetts Garden is an informal Victorian garden set on Ide Hill, at 700 feet one of the highest spots in Kent. Here you will find rare trees and shrubs from across the world. Full of interest in

Spring, with profusely flowering shrubs and flowers, and in Autumn for Fall colours.

Emmetts was created between 1890-1927 by an Edwardian gentleman named Frederick Lubbock as a weekend retreat for his family. Lubbock was a friend of influential garden writer William Robinson and shared Robinson's enthusiasm for new and unusual plants. At Emmetts he decided to create a garden featuring exotic plants in a natural landscape.

Much of Emmetts is laid out on a sloping hillside, with views across the Kentish Weald and the North Downs. On a wooded slope you can walk through a small pinetum, an Alpine garden, and a south garden with exotic shrubs.

There are woodland walks through hillsides covered in bluebells in spring, and a longer walk brings you to the nearby National Trust property of Toy's Hill, one of the first Trust purchases. One of the prize trees at Emmetts is a giant Wellingtonia which is thought to be the tallest tree in Kent.

Godinton House and Gardens

Godinton is a lovely brick manor with roots going back to the 14th century. Godinton was for centuries the home of the Toke family, and much of the present house owes its form to work undertaken by Captain Nicholas Toke beginning in 1620.

The interior includes a stunning medieval great hall with a hammerbeam roof, and a 17th-century great chamber with ornate Georgian panelling.

History
The first house at Godinton may have been built around 1165. This date is shown on a stained glass window in the hall. The house was restored in 1448, around the time the Toke family came into possession of Godinton. In 1620-28 Nicholas Toke extended the medieval building to create an L-shaped manor house clad in red brick, with a symmetrical front facade in Dutch style.

He incorporated the medieval hall of the earlier house and retained fittings like the richly carved 1520s linenfold panelling and marble chimney pieces. There is more carved panelling from around 1630 in the Great Chamber. In the Chamber is a frieze showing soldiers drilling. Above the hall is the chapel, which was originally a solar, or private family quarters.

Though the great hall and great chamber deservedly get most of the attention at Godinton, there are other excellent period features, including a carved Jacobean staircase with heraldic beasts decorating the newel posts, and The White Room, with a plaster ceiling designed by Sir Reginald Blomfield. The interiors are full of fine furniture and historical collections of porcelain.

The house can only be viewed by guided tours, but you are then free to explore the 12 acres of gardens at your leisure. Unfortunately, we were not allowed to take interior photos on our visit, which is a shame because the house interiors are stunning.

Gardens

The gardens were designed by Blomfield in 1895 and are his first major garden commission. The result is primarily an Arts and Crafts layout, with separate garden rooms on varying colour schemes. From the formal gardens, you can look out onto the 18th-century parkland beyond.

Though the formality of the late Victorian design has been softened over time, the essentials remain, including formal yew hedges and topiary, water features and wide lawns, balanced by a wild garden, a walled garden still with its original greenhouses, a delphinium collection, rose garden, Italianate garden, and a profusion of daffodils in early spring.

Godinton is one of the best-kept secrets in Kent and deserves much greater attention. The gardens are among the finest in southern England, and the setting beside the lovely Jacobean mansion is wonderful.

Garden: Lovely formal and informal gardens surround the Jacobean manor of Godinton House. There is much variety here, including an 18th-century walled garden, Italianate garden, formal topiary, and a wild garden. Best in: spring, for daffodils and wildflowers in the Wild Garden.

Goodnestone Park Gardens

A well-restored modern garden offering a mix of formal and informal interest. The main features are the three-roomed walled garden, with arched views to the parish church. There is a woodland garden with winding paths beside a tranquil pool, and a formal parterre with views out over open parkland. In addition, there is an arboretum and Gravel Garden.

There are 15 acres of gardens, divided into several main areas. The most popular is the Walled Garden, with lovely views framing the nearby medieval church. Some of the walls that define the garden are older than the house, and contain a rose garden, rill garden, an alpine garden, ornamental greenhouse, and kitchen garden.

Beyond the walled garden is a woodland area, with winding trails through a mix of shrubs and trees, colourful with azaleas, camellias, and hydrangeas in summer. Earlier in the year this area is a sparkling with snowdrops, hellebores, and witch hazel.

Beside the house are formal terraces and parterres defined by box hedges and gravel paths. The parterre looks over the village cricket pitch, while steps lead up to a lime walk and yew hedges. The lime avenue leads to an arboretum, with numerous specimen trees. And speaking of trees, look for an ancient Cedar of Lebanon, which dates to the early 18th century. Other interesting tree varieties include the largest southern beech in the UK and examples of tulip trees and copper beech.

History
Address: Goodnestone Park, Goodnestone, Canterbury, Kent, England, CT3 1PL

The history of Goodnestone House goes back to at least the Tudor period when Sir Thomas Engeham had a manor house here. Later Engehams sold the property to the Bridges family, and in 1704 Sir Brook Bridges, 1st Baronet, built a new house in classical style. Soon after the house was built a large garden was laid out to a design by William Harris. Towards the end of the 18th century, these gardens were swept away by the 3rd Baronet in favour of a landscape park in the style then popular amongst country house owners.

The 3rd Baronet's daughter Elizabeth married Edward Austen, brother of novelist Jane Austen. Jane visited her brother and sister-in-law at Goodnestone House several times, and it was during a visit here in 1796 that she began writing 'Pride and Prejudice'. The 5th Baronet altered the house facade and added a series of formal terraced lawns.

Though these historic beginnings helped lay the overall design of the gardens, it was not until the 1960s that work began in earnest to transform the landscape surrounding the house into what has been called one of Britain's finest gardens.

Great Comp Garden

Great Comp is a real plantsman's paradise, with great seasonal interest packed into 7 acres of formal and informal gardens. A feature of Great Comp are the 'ruins', follies which blend into the gardens and provide a focal point for the hardy and near-hardy plants which are the gardens main feature.

History
Address: Comp Lane, Platt, Sevenoaks, Kent, England, TN15 8QS

The gardens at Great Comp surround a picturesque 17th-century farmhouse, listed Grade II* for its historic interest. The house is built of lime-washed brick with stone dressings, and blocked up brick windows on the building's sides suggest a Tudor origin to the house. The interior features early 17th-century panelling and a late 17th-century staircase brought here from a farmhouse in Offham.

When Roderick and Joyce Cameron purchased the historic house in 1957 they decided to turn the grounds into a garden, beginning with 4.5 acres and later extended to 7 acres. They built an Italian garden, adding handmade 'follies' to create extra interest, using sand and stone from the garden itself. These 'ruins' are an important part of Great Comp, creating a focal point for exploring the gardens. A trio of classical urns, dubbed the 'Longleat Urn', 'Pope's Urn', and the 'Doulton Urn' act as focal points to emphasise points of view.

What to See

Near the manor house are formal gardens, while further away the sweeping lawns lead to a woodland area, where winding trails lead through beautifully planted trees and shrubs. Both formal and informal areas make careful use of statues and romantic follies to add interest to lush planting schemes.

Highlights of this densely planted plantsman's garden are over 30 varieties of magnolias, crocosmias, dahlias, and salvias. The magnolias and rhododendrons are at their best in spring and are underplanted with large drifts of bulbs and hellebores to add extra interest. In summer the warm colours dominate, especially the dahlias and fuchsias, mixed with ornamental grasses. But it's the salvias that are worth special mention; the gardens hold one of the finest salvia collections in Britain.

Roderick Cameron turned operation of Great Comp over to a charitable trust in 1992 and the Trust continues to maintain and develop the gardens. The Trust holds regular plant fairs as well as music and outdoor theatre events.

Groombridge Place Gardens

Peaceful 17th-century formal gardens surround a picturesque moated manor house at Groombridge Place, near Royal

Tunbridge Wells. Groombridge boasts a knot garden, white rose garden, oriental garden, peacock garden, herbaceous borders, and a secret garden, laid out as separate garden rooms.

History

The first written record of a manor house at Groombridge comes from 1239. William Russell built a moated fortified house here, with a later chantry chapel. The manor passed to the Cobham family, and then to the De Clintons, and at length to the Wallers of Lamberhurst.

Sir Richard Waller fought at Agincourt in 1415 and took Charles, Duke of Orleans prisoner. He held the Duke at Groombridge for several years, before he was eventually moved to the Tower of London.

The Wallers sold Groombridge in 1604 to Sir Thomas Sackville, 1st Earl of Dorset. Unfortunately, the 3rd Earl gambled his family fortune away and had to sell Groombridge to pay off his debts.

The buyer was John Packer, and it was his son Philip Packer who built the current manor in 1662. Packer was a friend of architect Sir Christopher Wren, and Wren helped design and build the new house.

Packer called upon another friend, horticulturist John Evelyn, to help design gardens to surround the house. Evelyn, more noted as a diarist, planted a pair of Scots pines by the bridge across the moat. He created a series of clearly defined garden rooms, blurring the boundaries between the house interior and the exterior.

A later writer, Sir Arthur Conan Doyle, was a visitor to Groombridge and modelled 'Birlstone Manor' in his Sherlock Holmes mystery 'The Valley of Fear' after the house. At the entrance to the formal gardens, you can visit the Conan Doyle Museum and Mini-Theatre, a tribute to the author and his connection to Groombridge.

A Secret Garden And A Romantic Mystery
One of the most intriguing garden areas at Groombridge is the Secret Garden, with a stream running through a quiet, hedged enclave. Philip Packer passed away in the Secret Garden while reading a book. A bit of a historical mystery clings to this garden as well.

The story goes that Richard Waller of Groombridge fell in love with Cecily Neville, wife of Richard Plantagenet and mother of Richard III.

When Cecily died in 1495 she was buried in the nearby churchyard and Waller planted a hawthorn tree beside her grave. A piece of the 'love tree' is kept in a box on the wall of the Secret Garden.

Unfortunately for this romantic story, it just can't be true, for the church had no burial ground in the 15th century, and Cecily Neville was buried at Fotheringhay in Northamptonshire.

A Smuggler's Tunnel
Philip Packer had heavy debts, and when he died the manor was held in Chancery. The house was deserted for 2 decades, and during this time an infamous group of smugglers known as the Groombridge Gang were active, and a persistent legend says that they built a tunnel from the Crown Inn, under the manor moat, to the cellars under the house.

The manor was later restored and is essentially unchanged since; an almost perfect example of a 17th-century manor.

Garden Highlights
Major garden features include a knot garden with displays of tulips, and the Apostles Walk, bordered by 12 yew trees planted in 1674. There is a herbaceous border with lush plantings of perennials, and Oriental garden with a theme of 'hot' colours,

and the Draughtsman's Lawn, where spring bulbs flourish and ornamental shrubs and trees offer vibrant colour in summer and autumn.

Other highlights include the Drunken Garden, one of Conan Doyle's favourites. The garden features yew and conifer topiary shaped to give he impression they are emerging from the mist organically. Perennial flowers and grasses are planted around a clock fountain.

The Knot Garden is rich with colourful tulips in spring and the white Rose Garden features over 20 varieties of roses underplanted with silver and white plants. A giant chessboard shelters under a yew tree planted by Sir Richard Waller in 1415 on his return from the Battle of Agincourt.

Aside from the gardens, there are a number of family attractions at Groombridge, including birds of prey, a zip wire, children's adventure playground, baby animals, and canal boat rides. Most of these family features can be found in the Enchanted Forest, which can be reached by a canal boat trip or a shaded walk along a peaceful waterway. Also in the Enchanted Forest is a Romany Camp with traditionally colourful wagons.

Hall Place and Gardens

Address: Bourne Road, Bexley, Kent, England, DA5 1PQ

Hall Place is a lovely manor house built in 1537 for a former Lord Mayor of London, Sir John Champneys. The interior boasts a very fine Tudor great hall with original panelling, overlooked by a minstrel's gallery. Look for the Queen's Beasts topiary garden, with hedges clipped to resemble heraldic symbols.

History

There was a manor house on this site in 1241, but the story of Hall Place really begins 3 centuries later when Sir John Champney, a former Lord Mayor of London, built a new house on a traditional Tudor plan, with a great hall acting as the centrepiece.

On one side of the hall were family quarters, with a great chamber and parlour, while on the other side was a service wing. Sir John Champney used stone from nearby Lesnes Abbey, which was dissolved a few years earlier by Henry VIII.

In 1649 the house was purchased by Robert Austen, a wealthy merchant from Tenterden. Austen set about transforming his new house, doubling its size by adding a new wing, with a staircase tower looking down on a red-brick courtyard.

Austen also added the Hall's most interesting interior feature, the ornate plasterwork ceiling that decorates the great chamber. Austen made no attempt to alter the style of the Tudor house, with the result that Hall Place looks like what it is; a house in two halves, representing 2 distinct time periods in English history.

In the 18th century, the house was bought by Sir Francis Dashwood, the most prominent member of the infamous Hellfire Club. The house served as a boarding school and was let to a succession of tenants. Then from 1860 Sir Francis' grandson Maitland Dashwood added a lodge and installed richly carved wooden panelling and parquet floors before letting the house once more.

The last tenant was the Countess of Limerick. It was Lady Limerick who planted the distinctive topiary garden of heraldic figures outside the house. Dubbed the 'Queen's Beasts', the topiary garden was opened to the public in honour of Elizabeth II's coronation.

World War Two brought dramatic changes to Hall Place when the U.S Army's Signal Corps 6811th Signal Service Detachment was stationed here. Beginning in 1944 the Corps helped British efforts to break the Enigma code machine used by the Germans, and tracked German Air Force signals. The American forces installed large numbers of radio receivers in the Great Hall and the Tudor Kitchen.

After the war was used by a girl's school, then by the local library and museum service for Bexley. The interiors were then restored and opened by the Bexley Heritage Trust.

Visitors can see the Great Hall and Tudor Kitchens, the Long Gallery, where objects from the museum are displayed, and the Chapel Gallery, with interactive displays for younger visitors. The interiors offer a marvellous glimpse of Tudor and 17th-century architecture, with period furnishings and wood panelling. When we visited there was a special exhibit on Hall Place during WWII, showing how the soldiers lived and worked here.

One of the most unusual items on show is a richly decorated free-standing shower installed by Lady Anne, located rather oddly at the top landing of the beautifuly carved staircase.

The house stands in 65 acres of gardens, with wildflower meadows mixing with more formal features like colourful herbaceous borders and topiary sculptures in the form of strange beasts. Visitors can see a wide range of wildlife including ring-necked parakeets and a kingfisher. The old walled gardens boast a subtropical glasshouse with rare and exotic plants.

Hall Place Today

The house is now owned by Bexley Heritage Trust, which also looks after nearby Danson House. Hall Place houses the Trust's museum, with over 50,000 objects related to Bexley heritage, from natural history and geology of the area, to archaeology, fashion, fine art and furniture.

A pair of special exhibits are arranged each year, displaying themed objects from the museum collection. There is also an extensive archive of local documents and photos to explore, in conjunction with the Bexley Local Studies and Archive Centre in Bexleyheath. There are regular special events, and the house can be hired for weddings.

Getting There

By far the easiest public transport acces to Hall Place is by rail to Bexley station. There are regular trains from London Bridge station to Bexley. From the station entrance walk north to Bexley High Street and turn right. Follow the High Street as it turns into Bourne Road, and take the overpass above the A2. You will see Hall pLace at the eastern end of the overpass. From the station to the Hall pLace entrance is roughly 15 minutes walk.

Garden: Formal topiary and herbaceous borders act as the setting for a fine Tudor manor. There is a secret garden and Italianate garden, plus a sub-tropical plant house and garden centre.

Historic Buildings in Kent

8 Palace Street

Address: 8 Palace Street, Canterbury, Kent, England, CT1 2DY

One of Canterbury's best half-timbered buildings. 8 Palace Street is a 13th-century building with later additions. It may have been built as the rectory for the nearby church of St Alphege.

The building is constructed with two projecting upper stories over a ground floor, each upper story projecting further than the last. The upper floors may be 15th century. It is also possible that the frontage we see facing onto Palace Street may have been brought in from another building.

The exterior is beautifully carved, with intricate floral and geometric designs rimming the jetties. The most intriguing features, however, are the carved brackets that support the jetties. These are in the shape of grinning demons, or grotesques, holding their bulging breasts in a pretty suggestive manner. Though one may be a female figure, the other is most definitely male.

NB. The house is private property, and is not generally open to visitors, though the carvings can easily be viewed from the street in front of the house. There are at least two further historic buildings further along Palace Street; Conquest House, and Sir John Boys House.

Blackfriars

Address: 25 High Street, Canterbury, Kent, England, CT1 2BD

The remains of a 13th-century friary, on the bank of the River Stour. Blackfriars was founded around 1237 by Dominican monks, whose black surcoat gave them the popular monicker 'Black Friars'.

Henry III granted the Black Friars land on an island in the River Stour. Here they built their new friary. There are only two buildings of the friary remaining; the guest hall, and the former rectory, which is now used by Kings College art centre.

The guest hall is best seen from St Peters Street, but one of the most enjoyable ways to view the Blackfriar's rectory is by taking a boat trip along the river. Regular trips leave from the Old Weavers House on St Peters Street during the summer months.

Canterbury City Walls

The Romans erected the first walls around Canterbury between 270 and 290 AD. Very little of those Roman walls remain. The walls we see today are medieval. The medieval walls surrounded the entire city of Canterbury and were pierced by eight gates, West Gate, North Gate, Quenin Gate, Burgate, Newingate, Riding Gate, Worth Gate, and London Gate. Of these, only West Gate remains.

West Gate Tower was erected by Archbishop Sudbury in 1380. It did nothing to increase his popularity; he was murdered by rioting peasants the following year. The West Gate is historically important as it represents one of the first defensive structures built with the use of gunpowder and artillery in mind. It uses keyhole gunports to create opportunities for cannon fire from a well-defended position.

The largest of the medieval gates was Riding Gate, which took traffic from the Dover road.

Several towers remain from the medieval fortifications. The most imposing of these is West Gate, but there are others in varying stages of repair, including Whitecross Tower, near Dane John Mound. Whitecross takes its name from a white stone cross set into the exterior stonework. This cross is in memory of Protestants burned at the stake during the dark years of the English Reformation at nearby Martyrs Field.

Near Burgate, there is another tower, now converted to use as a chapel. At the south end of the car park near Burgate is a stretch of Roman wall incorporated into the medieval stonework. Look for herringbone pattern stonework and rounded boulders and flints. The outline of Roman Queningate (c. 270-290 AD) can be seen blocked up near the current entry to the cathedral precinct. This gate was blocked up in 1492/3.

Between Queningate and North Gate are four square towers, erected by Prior Chillenden between 1390 and 1396.

The medieval walls form a rough oval about 3000 yards circumference. Note the use of keyhole gun ports at several locations along the wall. These are possibly the work of Henry Yevele, the master mason responsible for much of Bell Harry Tower at Canterbury Cathedral.

There were originally 21 mural towers set into the walls. Of these, 16 remain.

The best surviving section of the Roman wall is set into the rear of the Church of St Mary, Northgate. Here the walls still stand to 16 feet and are capped with original crenellations. There is a very well preserved section of Roman walling on St Radigund's Street, near the site of North Gate.

The city walls of Canterbury are among the best preserved in the country, and well worth a wander.

Canterbury West Gate Tower

Address: 2 St. Peters Street, Canterbury, Kent, England

One of the iconic landmarks of Canterbury, the old West Gate stands at the west end of the High Street, beside the River Stour. Generations of medieval pilgrims passed under the gatehouse arch on their way to the shrine of Thomas Becket at Canterbury Cathedral. Road traffic now flows through the arch - it's a bit of an eye-opener to see a modern coach navigate the narrow opening!

The West Gate was built by Archbishop Sudbury to replace an earlier Roman gate through the city walls. The West Gate was finished in 1380, but in the following year, Sudbury himself met a violent end at the hands of rebellious peasants during Wat Tyler's Peasant's Revolt.

For many years the West Gate served as the town prison, connected by a walkway to the police station next door. Above the portcullis slot is a 'condemned cell', where prisoners awaiting execution were held.

A bronze 18th-century medallion was found beneath the floorboards of the prison floor during recent repairs.

The upper floor of the gatehouse is given over to a small West Gate Museum. Here you will find armour and weapons used by defenders of Canterbury from the medieval period to World War II. Children can dress up in replica armour, and see the old prison cells within the gatehouse tower.

Immediately beside the tower is a lovely riverside garden, where you can take a punt tour along the River Stour.

Canterbury, St Alphege church

Address: Palace Street, Canterbury, Kent, England

St Alphege's was built around 1070 by Archbishop Lanfranc. It was rebuilt in the 12th century, and again in the 13th and 15th centuries. Among the interesting features is a late 15th-century pillar, funded by a bequest from Thomas Prude. A brass coat of arms has been set into the pillar, with the inscription, '*Gaude Prude Thoma per quem fit ista columna.*', which very loosely translates as 'Thomas Prude paid for this column'.

Thomas Cushman was married at St Alphege's. Cushman was responsible for hiring the *Mayflower*, the ship which took the Pilgrims to America in 1620. Cushman himself followed in 1621, but eventually returned to Britain, and died in Canterbury in 1625.

St Alphege ceased being used as a church in 1982, and for some time served as the home of the Canterbury Environmental Centre. It is now used by King's School, and the interior is not generally open to the public.

Within the church is buried John Caxton, brother of printing pioneer William Caxton of Tenterden. The font is hexagonal and dates from the 15th century.

St Alphege was an 11th-century Archbishop of Canterbury. When Danes under Earl Thorkell invaded in 1011 they took Alphege captive. The witan (council) agreed to pay the Danes £84,000, a huge sum in those days, to leave. The Danes wanted an extra £3000 to free Alphege, but the Archbishop urged his countrymen to refuse the ransom. The Danes killed Alphege in a rage by throwing beef bones at him. He was eventually buried in Canterbury Cathedral, near the high altar.

Charing Palace

Charing Palace is the remains of an 11th-century bishops palace used by Archbishops of Canterbury as a stopping place between Canterbury and their London residence of Lambeth Palace. The village of Charing stood on the main pilgrim route to Canterbury, and it made sense for the Archbishop's to have an official presence there.

The name 'palace' is perhaps a misnomer; the bishop's residence was really a manor house, albeit a very grand one, as befitted the status of the Archbishops of Canterbury.

The history of the palace goes back to the 8th century. In AD 788 Kenulph of Kent granted land at Charing to Christchurch Priory at Canterbury to build a residence. The residence evolved over the centuries into a complex of buildings based around a hall. It became a favoured residence of several archbishops.

Many of the medieval buildings that made up the Palace still survive as private dwellings. The boundary wall that enclosed the Archbishop's precinct still stands to a height of 2 metres high in places, and within it, the interior buildings remain relatively unaltered by the passage of time.

Most of the Palace buildings date to the 14th century, including the Great Hall, gatehouse, farmhouse, part of the west range, and part of a private chapel.

On the south side of the boundary wall is an imposing gatehouse built by Archbishop John Stratford (1333-1348). The gateway gives access to a courtyard, with buildings ranged around a quadrangle. On the east side of the courtyard is the 14th century Great Hall, later used as a barn. On the north side is the farmhouse, begun in the 13th century. At one corner stand the chapel remains.

On the west side of the courtyard is a 14th-century outbuilding, and on the south side are Numbers 1 and 2, Palace Cottages, the former gatehouse and porter's lodge.

It is thought that both Henry VII and Henry VIII stayed at the palace on numerous occasions. In 1520 the Palace hosted some of the 4000 men and women of Henry VIII's entourage as they journeyed to the king's famous meeting with Francis I of France at the Field of the Cloth of Gold near Calais.

The Charing estate remained in the hands of Canterbury Priory until 1545 when Archbishop Cranmer exchanged it with Henry VIII. It seems that Henry VIII made no use of the palace after he acquired it. The crown rented out the manor house, which became a farmhouse.

In 1559 Archbishop Parker tried to reassert church control over the palace and become both tenant and farmer of the Charing estate but the palace was instead sold to Sir Richard Sackville. It has been in private hands ever since.

By tradition whenever an Archbishop of Canterbury visits Charing he enrobes at the Palace (by permission of the current owner) before walking to the neighbouring parish church.

Part of Charing Palace was used for many years as a farm building, but attempts have been made recently to obtain funding for restoration. The various buildings are in private hands as this is written, and not generally open to the public, but you can easily view the precinct wall and poke your nose inside the gatehouse to see the historic complex of buildings arranged around the courtyard. It is an incredibly impressive site, with a marvellous sense of history.

Christ Church Gateway

Address: The Precincts, Canterbury, Kent, England

The main visitor entrance to Canterbury Cathedral precinct is through this highly decorated gateway, which was originally built to celebrate the marriage of Arthur, Prince of Wales, to Catherine of Aragon in 1502. Arthur, unfortunately, died a few months later, and the gate was not finished for another 20 years.

It was worth the wait, however, as Christ Church Gateway is an extraordinary monument; it is highly embellished and decorated with heraldic motifs, including coats of arms and mythical beasts.

At the centre, above the gateway arch, is a very large figure of Christ. This is a modern statue, replacing the original statue which was damaged during the Civil War by Parliamentary troops. Apparently, the troops decided to use the statue for target practice, then, not content with the damage they had inflicted, attached ropes to the statue and pulled it down.

There are two doors through the gate; a large door to the right, and a much smaller portal to the left. Both doors are beautifully carved and embellished with more heraldic symbols.

Christ Church Gateway has been the subject of numerous paintings over the years, including several by JMW Turner which can be seen in the Fitzwilliam Museum in Cambridge and the Tate Gallery in London.

Cobham Mausoleum

The Darnley family of Cobham Hall in Kent were traditionally buried at Westminster Abbey, a fitting final resting place for the influential family. However, when the 3rd Earl died in 1781 the vaults at Westminster were full.

In his will, the Earl asked for a family mausoleum to be built in the old deer park surrounding the Hall. The Earl had gone on a Grand Tour in his youth and was heavily influenced by the art and architecture he encountered in Italy. He asked that the mausoleum have a prominent pyramid and be surrounded by a dry moat.

The 4th Earl complied with his father's wishes, and architect James Wyatt drew up plans for an ornate neo-classical mausoleum along the lines of a Roman temple.

Wyatt even displayed his plans to the Royal Academy in 1783, but his schedule was too busy to allow him to take charge of construction (given his dubious reputation for quality control that's perhaps just as well). Construction was executed by George Dance the Younger in 1786, and the result was a slightly modified version of Wyatt's plan. The final cost was in the region of £9000, roughly equivalent to £1 million today.

The Mausoleum is square with projecting corners, and rises to a pyramid-shaped top. The exterior is Portland stone, and the style is that of a Roman temple, with Doric columns and classically inspired carving details. The unusual pyramidal roof, however, has no precedent in classical Roman style, and was possibly inspired by a romanticised painting by Nicholas Poussin rather than any actual Roman building.

Access is by a flying staircase, leading to a piano nobile, or inner chamber. At the far side of the chamber is an ornate chapel area of rose marble, rising to a domed ceiling above. Around the rear of the Mausoleum, a flight of steps descends to a vaulted crypt lined with openings for 32 coffins.

An Empty Shell

Though the mausoleum was completed, no burials ever took there. The reason for this oddity is unclear, but one possibility is that the Earl fell out with the Bishop of Rochester, so the Bishop refused to consecrate the building.

In the 1790s landscape architect Humphry Repton was called in by the 4th Earl to create a picturesque landscape garden from the parkland surrounding Cobham Hall. Repton wanted to turn the Mausoleum into a viewing platform, but the Earl refused. Repton's final design made the mausoleum an important focal point, not surprising given its prominent position on a hill high above the Hall.

The Darnley family sold the Hall in the 1950s, and it is now a popular school. The family kept the woods and mausoleum, however, but after a period of neglect, when the Mausoleum suffered badly from vandalism, they eventually sold the property to Gravesend Council in 2001.

It was restored with the aide of some original Wyatt drawings and plans are underway to restore the surrounding Cobham

Woods to Repton's design. You can see 'before' and 'after' photos inside the Mausoleum, and it is quite astonishing to see how the building has been brought back from a decrepit shell to the elegant monument we see today.

Visiting

There is a small parking area on Lodge Lane, at the eastern edge of Cobham village. From there a path leads past a lovely thatched cottage and straight through Cobham Park, rising steadily until you reach the Mausoleum. On a clear day the view is stunning, and it is easy to see why Repton's landscape garden made the building such a prominent focal point.

When we visited there were very helpful National Trust volunteers in the piano nobile and in the crypt and they told us the story of the building and the curious mystery of why it was never used for burials. I left with many a backward glance - and many a photograph - for the Mausoleum is one of the most striking neo-classical buildings I've ever visited.

Conduit House

Address: Kings Park, Canterbury, Kent, England, CT1 1TF

Conduit House is a wide circular cistern in the ground, with a set of pipes running into it from several directions. The conduit house gathered water from the hillside above the abbey and then sent it through further pipes down the hill to the abbey site. Water was carried through 3-inch lead pipes and fed into a water tower at the abbey. From the tower, it flowed into smaller tanks serving the kitchen, infirmary, and other parts of the monastery.

The same group of springs supplied water for other locations in the town. Canterbury Cathedral, for one, used the same water supply. There were several more water conduit houses and collection tanks taking water from the same source.

The Conduit House continued in use after the Abbey was suppressed by Henry VIII and supplied water for a local brewery into the 19th century.

A good source of clean water was essential for monasteries, and monastic houses were often established with water in mind. Monasteries located in towns faced a more serious problem and often had to bring in water from great distances, relying on a conduit house, or covered settling tank, to gather spring water and carry it to the site by means of long pipes.

St Augustine's Abbey's conduit house was built in the 12th century. The roughly octagonal masonry settling tank is now divided by an 18th-century wall made of brick and chalk. Seven openings admit water from springs into the tank. There are four large arched openings and three smaller ducts.

The water tank is made of chalk and flint set on chalk foundations. The inner face of the walls is made of coursed flint and was originally covered with render. The tank bed is chalk, whose high clay content keeps the water from flowing through.

In the 18th century, the medieval tank was subdivided and a new roof built, supported by two barrel vaults. The remodelling was probably the work of Sir John Hales, who owned the water supply. In 1773 Hales granted the city of Canterbury the right to use the holding tank to augment its own water supply. That 18th-century conduit house roof collapsed in 1988, leaving the original medieval tank and tunnels in view.

The Conduit House is right beside the Stour Valley Walk, a long-distance path that leads through Canterbury along the Stour River valley.

It takes about 10 minutes to walk to the Conduit House from the abbey site. Be aware that it is not well signposted!

Conquest House

On 29 December 1170, four knights, Reginald FitzUrse, Hugh de Moreville, William de Tracy, and Richard le Breton, met at a house near Canterbury Cathedral to plan what they would do on the morrow. Whatever plan they discussed, the result was the murder of Thomas Becket, Archbishop of Canterbury, a deed which changed the course of history and certainly changed the fortunes of Canterbury itself. The place where the knights met is reputed to be Conquest House on Palace Street.

At that time Conquest House was owned by a man called Gilbert the Citizen. The knights initially left their servants and weapons in Conquest House while two of their number entered Bishop's Palace by force and remonstrated with Becket, trying to get him to remove the excommunication he had placed over several of the king's supporters.

It was a lost cause from the start; Becket was too strong-willed to succumb to their threats. The knights returned to Conquest House and gathered their weapons. In the meantime, the archbishop's servants convinced him to retire to the cathedral. It was no use; the knights entered the cathedral, and after a further argument, killed Becket in the area now called The Martyrdom.

Looking at Conquest House (now an art gallery and function room) today it is hard to think of it as a 12th-century building. The front that greets your eye as you pass down Palace Street is an enormously attractive half-timbered facade in late Tudor or Jacobean style.

As attractive as the house exterior looks - and it certainly is attractive - it hides a much older interior, for behind the timber-framing lies a Norman undercroft. By comparison, the 14th-century galleried hall is relatively modern to say nothing of a highly decorative 17th-century fireplace!

There are several interesting carvings, including an ornate coat of arms over the fireplace, created to celebrate the marriage of Charles I to Henrietta Maria, which took place at Canterbury Cathedral in 1625.

The exterior of Conquest House is beautifully embellished with carvings, including a decorative frieze along the eaves, and fanciful brackets supporting the projecting jetties that thrust out over Palace Street.

Museums to visit in Kent

Beaney House of Art and Knowledge

Address: 18 High Street, Canterbury, Kent, England, CT1 2RA

The Beaney House of Art and Knowledge (formerly the Royal Museum and Art Gallery with the Buffs Museum) is housed in the former Beaney Institute building on High Street. This delightful Grade II listed Victorian building was founded by Dr James Beaney, a Canterbury physician who later emigrated to Australia where he became so rich he was known as 'Diamond Jimmy'.

The Art Gallery
The gallery is the major local venue for art, both modern and historical. In addition, the gallery is used as a venue for the performing arts. A special gallery is devoted to the work of artist Thomas Sidney Cooper, famed for his portraits of cattle.

Beaney Museum
Within the museum are collections of Old Master drawings, paintings dating to the 16th century, local archaeological artefacts, and Saxon jewellery from the region. There is a Geological and Natural History Collection, prehistoric tools, 5th-century rune stones. A fascinating artefact is St Augustine's

Chair, traditionally said to have been the seat used by Augustine when he received British bishops.

NB. Don't confuse this 'St Augustine's Chair' with the marble 'cathedra' or archbishop's chair in the cathedral!

There are a collection of drawings by Thomas Sidney Cooper, examples of Dutch stained glass, and finds from Ancient Egypt. One highlight is the collection of Greek Art gathered by Viscount Strangford.

Buffs Regimental Museum

A special gallery within the museum building houses the regimental collection of The Buffs (formerly the Royal East Kent Regiment). The collections include items loaned from the National Army Museum in London.

The Beaney Institute also houses an extensive local library containing historic documents dating to the 17th and 18th centuries. Among these are old maps, illustrations, and local newspapers.

Canterbury Roman Museum

Address: 11a Butchery Lane, Canterbury, Kent, England, CT1 2JR

This museum contains excavated sections of the old Roman town of Canterbury, including sections of a Roman town house with a well-preserved mosaic. In addition, there are audio-visual aids and hands-on activities designed to give visitors a real feeling for how the Romans lived in Canterbury.

There is a scale reconstruction of a Roman market place, with a fruit seller, fabric maker, and shoemaker selling their wares.

There is also an archaeological database showing details of Roman finds in and around the city of Canterbury.

There are regular events at the museum, allowing visitors to do such activities as make a Roman bracelet or hammer out a coin.

Chart Gunpowder Mills

Address: Fleur de Lis Heritage Centre, Stonebridge Way, Faversham, Kent, England, ME13 8NS

One of the few remaining gunpowder mills in the UK, Chart Mill was the home of English gunpowder manufacture for centuries, from its initial construction around 1560 until the 1930s. The current mill was built in the 18th century and provides a fascinating look into the painstaking production of explosives and gunpowder over time. Seasonal opening.

The mill was closed in the 1930s and faced demolition until it was rescued by the Faversham Society, who restored the buildings and machinery and opened it to the public in 1969.

Chart Gunpowder Mill was used to 'incorporate', or combine, the mixture of saltpetre, sulphur and charcoal used to create gunpowder. This painstaking process involved 11 distinct stages, and was, as you might assume, quite dangerous if any of the steps were not performed precisely. There were originally 2 wheels driving 4 mills, but now only one iron wheel is active.

Cranbrook Museum

Address: Carriers Road, Cranbrook, Kent, England, TN17 3JX

The Cranbrook Museum is a museum of local history for Cranbrook and area, housed in a historic 15th-century timber-framed farmhouse. Collections include Cranbrook Town, Rural Industry, Agricultural Tools Kitchen and Scullery displays, Military history, historic costumes, and much more. The museum is set in attractive gardens.

The Historic House

The picturesque museum building was built around 1480 as a home for the bailiff of Rectory Farm, which was owned by the

Archbishop of Canterbury. The bailiff's home took the form of a traditional hall house. Original medieval features include moulded timber posts and a beam carved with the likeness of a dragon. The house was later rented out to tenants. One 16th-century tenant was Richard Taylor, a wealthy clothier.

Shortly after 1620, the medieval hall house was rebuilt. Two chimney stacks were inserted, each with an inglenook fireplace. The building was in use as a vicarage throughout the 17th century. One resident was Rev Charles Buck, the vicar of Cranbrook. In 1683 Rev Buck added brick facing on the north and west sides of the house The date is inscribed in the exterior plasterwork.

In the Victorian period, the house was divided into four separate cottages. In the 20th century, the house was acquired by the Cranbrook Rural District Council, and in 1971 the Council made one of the cottages available to the Cranbrook Museum & Local History Society to act as its museum. Over the following 24 years, the museum expanded into the other cottages as tenants left until in 1995 the whole building was restored and given over to full-time use as a museum.

The Museum

The museum holds over 6,000 items of local heritage interest. There are special exhibits on local churches and schools, family life, rope-making, old coinage, bootmaking, farming, local trades and tradesmen, bygone industries, social history, and the 'Cranbrook Colony' of artists.

The Cranbrook Colony was a group of artists who began to settle in the Cranbrook area around 1854. The Colony focussed on painting scenes of everyday life, with themes of family, childhood, religion, working life, ageing and death. The first artist to make his home in Cranbrook was Frederick Hardy who settled in a house on High Street.

He was joined in 1857 by Thomas Webster, who acted as Hardy's mentor. They set up their studio in Hardy's house, and he lived in the basement. The pair were quickly joined by fellow artists George Hardy (Frederick's brother) John Horsely, and George O'Neill (who was married to Horsely's cousin). The artists were very active in community life and gave generously to local causes. A memorial to Thomas Webster stands in Cranbrook's parish church.

Researchers of family history will enjoy the extensive collection of local archives. The artwork on display includes several paintings by William Jones Chapman (1808-1870).

The Museum is managed by the Cranbrook Museum & Local History Society, which publishes a number of fascinating books relating to Cranbrook local history as well as an annual journal.

Dover Museum

Address: Market Square, Dover, Kent, England, CT16 1PH

The Dover Museum traces the story of Dover from prehistoric times to the present day. Exhibits cover Dover town and port and include Roman history, Dover's role as a member of the Cinque Ports, Napoleonic and Victorian Dover, and the history of Dover during both World Wars.

Perhaps the most intriguing historic artefact on display is the so-called 'Dover Bronze Age Boat', an ancient boat that is probably the oldest seagoing vessel anywhere in the world. The boat which was discovered in Dover in 1992, dates from over 3550 years ago. The boat is the centrepiece of an award-winning gallery showcasing local archaeology, and including Bronze Age finds from across Kent.

There are plenty of hands-on activities and audio-visual tools for capturing children's imaginations.

Dover Museum is among the oldest museums in Kent. It was built in 1836 and rehoused in 1991 in a completely new building hidden behind the original Victorian facade.

Visiting Dover Museum
It is easy to find the museum; it is located on one side of the Market Square and is very well signposted (look for the 'Bronze Age Boat' brown tourist signs). There is a paid parking area about five minutes level walk - also very well signposted. It is worth noting that when we visited there was a half-price deal for English Heritage members, so that was handy.

The Bronze Age Boat
Though the exhibits offer a very enjoyable look at Dover over the centuries, it is the Bronze Age Boat exhibit that really is the star of the show. I was honestly unprepared for just how impressive the boat is. The more I looked at it the more awed I became; the skill of construction and size of the vessel is simply incredible.

There were very interesting displays showing how the vessel was built and how archaeologists think it looked. You can even try your hand at tying a special knot that the builders used to keep the timbers tight.

We were fortunate enough to arrive at the boat exhibit during a talk given by an expert to a local group of visitors, and it was fascinating to eavesdrop and get a better sense of why and how the boat was built, and realise just how amazingly well it was preserved through the centuries by being encased in mud. I highly recommend taking the time to visit the museum and the boat exhibit.

Finchcocks

Address: Goudhurst, Kent, England, TN17 1HH

Finchcocks bills itself as the '*Living Museum of Music*'. The Richard Burnett Collection of historic keyboard instruments is set in the lovely surroundings of a beautiful Georgian manor house in the Kent countryside. There are over 70 keyboards on display, with the majority dating from the late 18th and early 19th century. Among the collection is a piano owned by Prince Albert.

Finchcocks was built in 1725 by Edward Bathurst, a wealthy lawyer. His vision was to create a mansion 'of great expense and in a stately manner'. With a budget of £30,000, he was able to realise his vision, but we aren't sure which architect helped him do it.

The design has been variously attributed to Thomas Archer and John Vanbrugh, but it seems just as likely it was the work of an unknown local builder using one of a number of popular 'pattern books'. These pattern books were essentially architectural drawings in fashionable style, much like a home design magazine we might see today, but illustrated in fine detail, with elegantly drawn views of architectural details.

The design was long and thin, only one room thick in the central block, so that the house looks larger from the outside than it really is. The effect is enhanced by a grandiose central portico and Baroque facade. Despite the external grandeur, the original house boasts but 20 rooms, fairly small in the country house scheme of things.

Interior furnishings are pure 18th century as if the house has been lost in time for almost 300 years. Indeed, Finchcocks was very slow to acquire the most essential modern inventions; indoor plumbing and heating were only added in 1920.

But it is not the Georgian furnishings that will draw visitors, it is the collection of historic musical instruments for which

Finchcocks is famous. There are over 100 keyboard instruments, 40 of them are in full working order.

Included are pianos, harpsichords, clavichords, organs, and oddities such as an 1870 'digitorium', a crystallophone, barrel organ, and music boxes. One of the more unusual pieces is a lyre piano, which is exactly what it sounds like - a combination lyre and keyboard. Staff are on hand to give demonstrations.

Aside from the keyboards, Finchcocks has an exhaustive collection of prints depicting London pleasure gardens during the 18th century.

Aside from regular open days, there is an ongoing programme of daytime and evening concerts throughout the year.

Historic Dockyard Chatham

Chatham Historic Dockyard, on the River Medway in Kent, built warships from the time of Henry VIII. Restored vessels on display include HMS Gannet, the last sloop of Queen Victoria's Royal Navy, historic warship HMS Cavalier and the submarine Ocelot.

History

Around the year 1547, the Royal Navy began to use the stretch of the River Medway around Chatham for a pair of storage depots. By the reign of Elizabeth I Chatham was the major fleet base, and most of the navy vessels overwintered here. In 1570 a boatyard was begun at Sunne Hard to repair and maintain vessels in the Medway. The first ship to be built in the new yards was the Sunne, launched in 1586.

Only 2 short years later the shipwrights of Chatham were called on to help prepare England to face the might of the Spanish Armada. Most of the fleet that faced the Armada sailed from the Medway under the command of Lord Howard of Effingham, Elizabeth's Lord High Admiral. The Elizabethan dockyards were moved from Sunne Hard to the current location in Chatham in 1613, and no trace of the earlier site remains.

The core of the new dockyards were large drydocks, where new boats could be built, and existing ships maintained. The area around the drydocks developed into a huge complex of buildings, each fulfilling a special task. There were drying areas for masts, rope-making areas, carpentry areas, plus residences for officers and naval officials. The yards employed thousands of skilled craftsmen and must have been an amazing place, bustling with noise and activity.

By the middle of the 18th century, the Royal Yards had become the largest industrial organisation in the world. It would not be too much of a stretch to claim that it was the skilled craftsmen of Chatham that were responsible for Britain's dominance of the seas.

Yet the prosperity at Chatham would not last; as British focus shifted away from the North Sea and the Channel to the Mediterranean and the Americas. The dockyards at Portsmouth and Plymouth better suited Britain's new role as a world sea power, and at the same time, the River Medway began to silt up. Chatham stopped being a base for the fleet and became instead a centre for repair and shipbuilding.

Perhaps the most famous ship to be built in the Chatham Dockyards was the HMS Victory, launched in 1765. The Victory was repaired here in 1797 and returned to sea in time to serve as Admiral Nelson's flagship at the Battle of Trafalgar in 1805.

The construction of sailing ships ceased in 1849 and the first screw-powered ship to be built at Chatham, the Horatio, launched in 1850. The 20th century saw a new stage, as attention at Chatham focussed on submarines. In total, 57 submarines were built here from 1908 until production ceased in 1960.

No. 1 Smithery

Set aside as a special museum area, with exhibits from the Imperial War Museum and the Royal Museums at Greenwich. On display are a wealth of scale ship models, paintings, and memorabilia. A Maritime Treasures Gallery displays naval art, and ship models, while the Pipebending floor shows how metal pipes were bent around pegs in the floor to make them fit the requirements of individual vessels.

Hearts Of Oak

This very large display area contains a museum of Chatham's role in Britain's naval history. See how some of the most famous vessels in our maritime history were built, with an emphasis on sail-powered, wooden-hulled warships. The gallery is themed around the story of a retired Master Shipwright named John North as he relives his career and encourages his grandson to follow in his footsteps.

Steam, Steel, And Submarines

This area of the Dockyards covers the history of Chatham through the turmoil of the Industrial Revolution, to the First, and Second World Wars. It spans the era from the launch of the first steam-powered ship, the Phoenix, in 1832, to the Okanagan, a submarine built for the Canadian navy in 1966.

The Victorian Ropery

One of the most popular areas of the Dockyards is this fascinating workshop. Rope was essential for sailing ships, and has been made at Chatham since 1618. A tour with costumed guides walks you through the process of rope making, and you can try your hand at traditional rope-making tools and techniques. The end of the tour is the ropewalk, which stretches fully 1/4 mile and still has its working Victorian equipment.

Hms Gannet

This restored sloop was built in 1878 and was powered both by steam and sail. The hull is made of teak planks wrapped around an iron frame.

The Gannet was part of Britain's policy of 'gunboat diplomacy' in the last quarter of the 19th century, when Britain's worldwide Empire was protected and trade efforts strengthened with a strong naval presence. But enforcing Britain's naval prominence was not the Gannet's only role; she was meant to clamp down on slavery and piracy and at the same time chart the seas she sailed for the Admiralty's maps. The Gannet saw action just once in her long career; at Suakin, in 1886. The ship has now been restored to the way she was fitted out at that time.

Hms Cavalier

Built in 1944, the Cavalier was the last WWII destroyer to see action. It is preserved at Chatham as a memorial to the 11,000 men lost at sea in the war, and the 142 British destroyers sunk during the conflict. The Cavalier served in the Arctic and the Western Approaches before joining the Pacific Fleet. The ship sailed with the Far East Fleet and the Home Fleet until she was retired in 1972. Visitors can explore every corner of the restored vessel in a free-flow tour.

Hm Submarine Ocelot

The last warship built at Chatham, the Ocelot launched in 1962. She is an 'O' class vessel, powered by diesel-electric engines. She saw service throughout the Cold War and was retired in 1991. The ship was manned by a crew of 69 - and frankly, they were cramped!

The Ocelot is the only one of the three historic vessels at Chatham that must be accessed by a guided tour. These tours are very popular, so I recommend you book a tour time as soon as you enter the Dockyards! The interior of the submarine is extremely cramped, but navigating the interior of the vessel on a tour really brings home what life must have been like for the crew. It's an eye-opening experience.

Commissioner's House

This elegant building was erected in 1704 as a residence for the Dockyard's commissioner Captain George St Lo. It is the oldest intact naval building in Britain and stands on the site of an even earlier building. Behind the House is a garden laid out in the 1640s.

Rnli Historic Lifeboat Collection

Seventeen lifeboats are displayed in this fascinating exhibit. Relive the perilous tale of some of the RNLI's most famous and difficult rescues.

Visiting

There is just so much history at Chatham it is almost too much to take in! Please give yourself plenty of time to explore the entire site. This is a vast historic site where you will want to take your time - and I guarantee you'll still end up missing something you wanted to see! I highly recommend booking tours for the historic vessels. The Victorian Ropery is also interesting, and don't miss the Assistant Harbour Master's House, built in 1770, and the ceremonial water gate behind it where visiting dignitaries came ashore.

Kent Museum of the Moving Image

Address: 41 Stanhope Road, Deal, Kent, England, CT14 6AD

Celebrating 350 years of the moving and projected image', that's the tagline of the Kent Museum of the Moving Image (MOMI) in Deal. The museum covers much more than the history of modern filmmaking, delving back into the heritage of projected images to see where our fascination with moving images began. Think of MOMI as a combination of a cinema museum and a 'pre-cinema' museum.

MOMI's mission is to be a combination museum, archive, research library, entertainment venue and hands-on 'exploratorium' for the moving image in all its forms. It aims to be both a fun family day out and a serious resource for students of cinema history.

But when did the 'prehistory' of the moving image begin?

You could make the claim, as MOMI does in its '35,000 Years to Catch a Shadow' exhibit, that the story really begins with the first cave paintings.

Leonardo Da Vinci proposed the concept of a projection system, but things didn't take off until the invention of the telescope and the microscope in the early 17th century. These two inventions fostered a huge interest in the science of optics and prompted the invention of the magic lantern - light shown through a painted slide to create an image outline against a solid surface.

The museum looks at our earliest attempts to project images with 'magic lanterns' lit by candles, projecting images of hand-painted slides.

Magic lanterns were fascinating, but only the wealthiest people could afford them. One of MOMI's prize exhibits is an 1890 triple-lens magic lantern projector, complete with a set of original magic lantern slides. The projector is maintained in full working order and still has its original travelling trunk.

Delve into the history of London's 'Polytechnic Institute', a palatial multimedia centre where crowds thronged to watch magic lantern shows in the very first purpose-built projection theatre. The 'Poly' as it was popularly known, offered visitors much more than magic lantern shows; they could enjoy kaleidoscopes, photographs, 3-D stereoscopes illustrated newspapers and optical toys.

All of MOMI's exhibits are unique. Or to put it another way, every exhibit is a special exhibit, so that there is always something new to see.

Recent exhibits include a retrospective on Ealing Studios, covering both the films produced at Ealing and the iconic posters used to promote them.

The museum has a cafe and shop. There is no onsite parking, aside from limited parking for disabled access, available by pre-arrangement.

Maidstone Museum & Bentlif Art Gallery

Address: St Faith's Street, Maidstone, Kent, England, ME14 1LH

The Maidstone Museum first opened its doors in 1858, but the location has a much longer history, for the museum is housed in Chillington Manor, a historic Elizabethan manor house that dates back to 1562. The Cloisters and Long Gallery date even further back to an earlier Tudor building. The manor was given to the town of Maidstone in 1855 by Thomas Charles, a successful surgeon and antiquarian.

The museum has expanded since those early days to include over 660,000 artefacts covering a wide range of subjects. Among the museum galleries are exhibits covering Ancient Egypt, Archaeology, Costume, Ethnography, Biology, Fine & Decorative Art, Geology, and Local History. There is also a special section on Japanese Decorative Arts & Prints. There is also an ongoing programme of special events.

A special wing added to the east side of the old manor house houses the Bentlif Art Gallery, founded by a bequest from Samuel Bentlif in honour of his brother George. The gallery began with 200 paintings donated by Bentlif.

The collection of fine art deserves special mention; with 574 oil paintings, it is the largest publicly owned collection in Kent and includes several Italian Old Masters. Also located within the Maidstone Museum is The Queens Own Royal West Kent Regiment Museum.

As of this writing, the museum is open without admission charge every day except Christmas, Boxing Day, and New Years Day.

Powell-Cotton Museum, Quex House and Gardens

The stately home of Quex House is home to the Powell-Cotton collection of African artefacts and natural history. Over the years 1885 to 1939 Major Percy Powell-Cotton and his family amassed an amazing collection of oddments, from mammals to carvings, covering Africa, India, and the Far East. Most of the collection is on display in a specially built museum beside the early 19th-century house, but the house itself is bursting at the seams with curiosities gathered from all over the globe.

In 1803 architect Thomas Hardwick designed a refined, elegant mansion for John Powell Powell. Though John had the house built, it is his descendent Major Percy Powell-Cotton who left his indelible mark upon Quex. Born in 1866, Powell-Cotton was the prototypical Victorian explorer. He led no fewer than 28 trips to Asia and Africa. Even his honeymoon was spent living with a tribe of African pygmies, and the newspapers made much of the fact that his new wife Hannah was the first European white woman 'in the land of the pygmies'.

Like many contemporary explorers, Powell-Cotton was an enthusiastic hunter, and, as Simon Jenkins rather graphically puts it in his 'England's Thousand Best Houses' book, 'he killed anything that moved'. On one occasion his enthusiasm for big game hunting almost resulted in his death, when a wounded lion charged him. He was saved by the actions of his porters, who managed to distract the lion from mauling the Major, and kill it.

Powell-Cotton was left with claw wounds and a badly torn suit, which is on display near the museum entrance.

The intrepid Major was not only a hunter but a pioneer in the use of photography to record animals in their natural habitat. He was one of the first wildlife photographers, using binocular lenses and glass-plate negatives to capture his images, and enthusiastically took up cine filming when the first 'moving picture' technology became available.

The end result of Powell-Cotton's explorations is a remarkable collection of over 500 cultural artefacts, stuffed and mounted animals, and mementoes of his travels. Among the items on show is an impressive collection of Chinese Ching dynasty Imperial porcelain. One of the things that really sets the Powell-Cotton collections apart is that the Major was a meticulous note-taker; he recorded in exacting detail the provenance of each cultural item and how it was used. The collection is fascinating for its cultural significance, but also for what it reveals about the late Victorian attitudes and values.

The house itself, though full of items collected by family travellers, is a comfortable Victorian home, all leather and genteel clutter. The exterior of the house dates from the 1880s but doesn't stray too far from the original 1803 design. The original house had a grand staircase of stone, but this was replaced by a wonderful oak stair. Upstairs rooms include a library, boudoir, and bedroom, much of it faithful to Hardwick's design. In the Library is a fascinating 'rolling ball' clock by Congreve, while at the top of the stairs is a 17th-century Italian marble bust of Democritus, 'The Laughing Philosopher', a gift of Lord Holland.

15 acres of gardens surround Quex House. Here you will find a Victorian walled garden, open lawns, exotic trees, woodland walks, and a wildlife pond. Also in the grounds - though not always open to view - is the extremely peculiar family mausoleum, built for John Powell Powell to house his collection of 12 bells. It is one of the very few secular bell towers in England still in use and is topped by a cage-like structure of cast iron that can best be described as something like the Eiffel Tower with a curving base, but in fact, it is modelled after the spire of Faversham church.

The house has limited opening hours but is well worth taking the time to view. And though the garden setting is wonderful, the real attraction for most visitors to Quex is the museum, which ought to be on every itinerary to south-east Kent!

Prehistoric sites in Kent

Bigbury Camp

Address: Bigbury Road, Harbledown, Kent, England, CT4 7LS

Bigbury Camp is an Iron Age hill fort that was the scene of British resistance against Julius Caesar in 54BC. The Romans subsequently used the hill fort as a military encampment site. Finds unearthed during excavations at Bigbury can be seen at both Canterbury and Maidstone museums.

The fort covers 26 acres (just under 11 hectares). Part of this area is a large enclosure to the north of the main fort that may have been used as a cattle pen. The main fort is enclosed by a 16-foot wide perimeter ditch with an earthwork bank on the inner lip.

Archaeological investigation found a series of post holes in the bottom of the ditch, suggesting that there was a timber palisade there for added security against attack.

There have been quite a few finds at Bigbury, including iron tools and kitchen implements, arrowheads, a knife, and a horse bridle.

One of the most intriguing finds was a slave chain, suggesting a trade in slaves between Britain and Gaul before the Roman period.

Battling The Romans
Bigbury was built around 350BC and was continuously occupied until Julius Caesar's invasion in 54AD. The Roman *Lego VII Claudia* attacked the hillfort, perhaps under Caesar's personal command, and scattered the native resistance. Caesar's history of the conquest records that the two fort entrances, one at the east and one at the west end, were reinforced by felled trees to block the Roman advance.

The First Canterbury?
After the battle, the inhabitants of Bigbury resettled around Canterbury, and it is quite possible that Canterbury was established as a new settlement specifically for people displaced by the Roman conquest at Bigbury.

The camp is located directly on the North Downs Way long-distance trail, and the Pilgrim's Way, which follow the same route at this point. If you are feeling like exercise it makes sense to reach the hillfort on foot as an afternoon outing from Canterbury.

Coldrum Longbarrow

Address: Coldrum Lane, Trottiscliffe, Kent, England, ME19 5EG

Coldrum Longbarrow is an almost intact Neolithic long barrow in the Medway Valley of Kent. The barrow is probably the best preserved in Kent; it measures an impressive 30 metres long by 18 metres wide (about 95 feet by 55 feet) and is surrounded by 15 sarsen stones arranged in a circle.

When the site was excavated in the early 20th century the bones of 22 people were found. These remains can now be seen at the Maidstone Museum.

The nearest car park is at Trottiscliffe, about 1/2 mile away, and footpaths lead to the site, which is accessible at any time. Fencing has been erected to prevent people from climbing on the stones, but you can approach quite close to the barrow.

Kit's Coty House

Address: Aylesford, Kent, England

Kit's Coty House is a dolmen burial chamber consisting of three upright stones and a capstone. The capstone is huge, about 4 metres by 2.7 metres in width. Nearby is Little Kit's Coty, also known as the Countless Stones.

Kit's Coty is oriented east to west, with a dummy entrance, or burial chamber, at the east end. It would have originally been covered in earth to create a large mound.

Visiting Kits Coty

To say that its a challenge to find Kits Coty is an understatement; its extremely difficult unless you happen to know where to look. There are no apparent signposts, at least none that we could find, and if it had not been for the assistance of a friendly local we found in the Lower Bell pub, we'd still be looking!

The dolmen is located just off the North Downs Way trail, in a field south of Chatham Road, immediately west of the A229, at grid reference TQ744608. There is no parking on Chatham Road itself, but as our local friend helped us out. Take the Old Chatham Road (signed Kits Coty Estate) and use a convenient layby just before it joins Chatham Road at its northern end.

The layby is at grid reference TQ746609. Cross Chatham Road to a set of stone steps with a railing where you can see a National Trails sign for the North Downs Way. The trail leads downhill through a shady tunnel of trees for 300 yards or so until you come to a gap in the trees to your right (west). You can see the dolmen through the gap in the trees.

Again, there is no signpost, but you really can't miss it. There is a small information plaque beside the dolmen, which is protected by a set of iron railings.

Little Kits Coty
A visit to Kits Coty can be combined with Little Kits Coty (the Countless Stones), which are about 400 yards away down the hill. Though the distance isn't great, it does require some determination!

To reach Little Kits Coty simply carry on down the hill, following the North Downs Way to a road junction. The trail crosses Rochester Road at an angle to your left, where you can see a sign labelled 'Pilgrims Way'. Technically you could carry on along Rochester Road to the south-west for 100 yards until you come to a brown English Heritage footpath sign, but the road is extremely busy, and there is no verge or footpath to speak of.

What we did was to follow the Pilgrims Way for 25 yards and then go through a gap in the hedge to a farm field. We walked along the edge of the field, parallel to Rochester Road, making for a belt of trees that jut out into the field. The burial site is inside the treed area, protected by an iron railing.

Please be careful to avoid damaging the field fencing and crops! It literally takes no more than 10 minutes to walk between the two burial sites; the major problem is simply knowing where they are and avoiding traffic when crossing roads!

Little Kit's Coty

Address: Aylesford, Kent, England

A prehistoric burial site, now little more than a confused jumble of sarsen stones. Little Kit's Coty stands about 450 metres south of the Kit's Coty House dolmen. This site is also known as Countless Stones.

Drawings by 18th-century antiquarian William Stukeley suggest that Little Kit's Coty may have been a long barrow. If so, there is no longer any evidence of a barrow on the site. There are several other standing stones in the area, and it has been suggested that these were the remains of similar burials or barrows.

Visiting Little Kits Coty House

Access to the site is theoretically easy; there is a short path off Rochester Road, signed by a brown English Heritage footpath sign. However, there is no parking area nearby, not even a convenient layby. Here's our suggestion: park on Old Chatham

Road, near its junction with Chatham Road, and follow the North Downs Way long-distance footpath to Kits Coty, then, once you've seen the dolmen, continue on down the hill for Little Kits Coty.

It makes for a longer trip - roughly 30-40 minutes to explore both sites and retrace your steps - but at least there's a safe place to park and you get to see both sites in one go. For a more detailed look at where to park and how to reach both sites see our article on Kits Coty House.

As for the site itself, though it is small and doesn't take long to explore, I actually found it rather intriguing. There are so many stones fallen in a large group that it is intriguing to work out how the site might have originally looked. Also, unlike many barrows, the Countless Stones were erected on flat land in a valley bottom, where most similar monuments were built on or near the brow of a hill.

Roman Sites in Kent

Lullingstone Roman Villa

Address: Lullingstone Lane, Eynsford, Kent, England, DA4 0JA

In 1939, on the eve of World War II, an exciting discovery was made in the low-lying fields beside the River Darent, just south of Eynsford, Kent. Remains of an extensive Roman villa were found, but it was not until after the war that a proper archaeological excavation revealed just how important the discovery really was.

For as investigators dug away the earth of centuries they uncovered the remains of a large villa with lovely mosaic floors depicting ancient myths. The mosaic at Lullingstone is among the finest ever found in England and is virtually complete and unaltered by time.

The Cult House and Chapel

Perhaps even more exciting than the mosaic was the discovery that one of the villa's chambers contained one of the earliest Christian chapels in the country, dating to the 4th century and situated above an earlier cult-house and a hypocaust. This chapel chamber was decorated with a chi-rho monogram, one of the earliest Christian symbols, and a set of wall paintings that were interpreted as showing Christians at prayer. The cult house has a niche in one wall with a painting of three water nymphs, so it seems quite likely the chamber was associated with a water cult.

Other chambers uncovered include sleeping quarters, kitchens, a porch or veranda, and a very extensive system of baths, with different pools for hot, warm, and cold baths.

But it is the mosaics that will draw most visitors; these decorate a large audience chamber and apse in the centre of the villa. The central figure depicted in the mosaic is Bellerophon riding the winged horse Pegasus and fighting the Chimera. The central figures are surrounded by four dolphins and two seashells, and these figures in turn are surrounded by foliage and geometric patterns. In the apse are further mosaics showing '*The Rape of Europa*'. In this scene Europa is abducted by the god Jupiter, disguised as a bull. The pair are flanked by winged figures, one of whom grasps the bull's tail.

The villa was begun around 75AD, at a time when the Romans had finally brought most of the unruly British tribes - at least those in the south and east - under their control, producing a period of relative peace and prosperity. The was rebuilt several times over the ensuing centuries until it was finally destroyed around 420AD, shortly after the last Roman legions left Britain for good.

The entire villa is contained in a large, modern visitor centre, with walkways at ground level and above, giving a bird-eye view of the whole site. There are exhibits of finds from the excavations at Lullingstone, and further displays on life in Roman Britain. Most of the displays seem aimed at a young audience; indeed, I'd say that English Heritage really emphasises the educational aspect of the remains over all others. But there are certainly interesting exhibits, including a pair of busts known, not surprisingly, as *The Lullingstone Busts*. One of these large sculptures is thought to represent a former owner of the villa. It also looks very similar to known busts of Pertinax, a governor of Britain who went on to become Emperor of Rome. Based on this circumstantial evidence, it is possible that Pertinax used the villa here as a country house, or retreat, during his tenure as governor.

Outside the visitor centre, on a raised bank of earth, is a small circular foundation wall in the turf showing the outline of a small 2nd century shrine. The shrine was excavated in the 1950s then recovered with earth to preserve the remains. Nearby, though not so readily visible, is the site of a mausoleum. After the departure of the Romans a Saxon chapel was erected over the site, but again, very little of this can be seen. Behind the villa/visitor centre is the site of a rectangular 2nd century kitchen, later used as a tannery. while in the field across from the car park was a large granary. Again, almost nothing of this building can be seen today.

Summing up Lullingstone

I found the villa fascinating, especially the cult house and chapel, and the mosaics were quite stunning. It was a little strange, to say the least, to have the entire villa under a huge roof, with coloured lights illuminating the excavated chambers like a *son et lumiere* show. I'd have to say that distracted a bit from getting a real feel for the site, but the exhibits were certainly interesting, including one rather poignant child burial display. I highly recommend combining a visit to the villa with the nearby historic house of Lullingstone Castle and the ruins of Eynsford Castle in the village.

Richborough Roman Fort

Address: Richborough Road, Richborough, Sandwich, Kent, England, CT13 9JW

A third-century Roman fortification with remains of a triumphal arch that may mark the spot where the Romans first came ashore for their successful AD 43 invasion of Britain. Later, an early Christian church was built within the walls of the Roman fort. There are inner and outer earthworks and extensive remains of fortifications. Richborough is memorable in that it was occupied from the successful Roman invasion of AD 43 until the departure of the Romans from Britain in AD 410.

History

At the time of the Roman invasion the area around Richborough looked very different to what it does today. At that time Richborough was an island in a natural lagoon at the southern end of the Wantsum Channel, linked to the mainland by a causeway. This created a natural harbour that was ideal for the invading Romans to establish a presence in southern Britain. Historical accounts do not make clear exactly where the Romans landed, but Richborough seems a prime candidate to be the 'Ritupaie' mentioned by historian Cassius Dio.

The first military fort here was quite basic; it was intended as a beachhead in enemy territory, not a permanent military camp. There are two parallel ditches which extend for almost 2200 feet, well beyond the present fort, and must have cut the Richborough promontory off from the mainland. There was an earth rampart on the seaward side of the ditches, and the site was entered through a timber gateway.

By the middle of the 1st century, Richborough was one of the primary supply bases for the army. It was only when the Romans had begun to establish control over Britain that Richborough changed its role. The final success of the invasion was marked by a large triumphal arch in the centre of the fort, at the junction of a crossroads. It is the arch that provides Richborough with one of its most intriguing features.

Though there is little of the actual arch remaining, the raised earthen banks, forming a large cruciform structure, and traces of foundation walls indicate a hugely impressive building, with decorated arches facing in four directions.

The Monumental Arch
Sometime around AD 85 the timber buildings used for the army supply base were torn down, making room for a large masonry gateway, symbolically representing a formal entrance to the new Roman province of Britain. Built at the junction of four roads, with an arch facing each road and a raised cross passage through the centre, the gateway was erected on a raised rectangular foundation of flint and mortar.

The gateway measured roughly 85 feet high and was constructed out of ashlar encased in Carrara marble imported from Italy. The gateway was richly decorated and had niches for bronze statues. So fine was the stonework that much of it was reused in building the west gate of the later fort after the gateway was destroyed.

The Mansio

The importance of Richborough as a supply base faded as the role of Dover increased, but the port and the town that grew up around it still thrived. One piece of evidence for the busy town is a mansio, or hotel for official visitors. There was a timber building on this spot in the 1st century, but during the 2nd century this was rebuilt in stone. When the 3rd-century fort was built the mansio fell out of use. a bath house was built on top of the earlier building, including a changing room, cold bath, warm bath, and hot room.

In the 3rd century defence became important once again, as the south coast came under threat from Saxon raiders. Around AD 250 an elaborate system of earthwork defenses was erected, and it is these concentric series of earthworks that gives Richborough its most eye-catching feature. The central area of the town was levelled to build an earthwork camp enclosing about 1 acre.

The earthen defences included three ditches and an internal rampart, accessed by a single gate on the western road Though most of the earlier buildings were demolished to make way for the new fort, the mansio was left untouched. In fact, the ditches seem to have been carefully aligned to avoid damage to the hotel. The monumental gateway was converted to use as a lookout. The first earthen fort lasted only about 25 years before the ditches were backfilled and the defences rebuilt in much more elaborate fashion, surrounded by high stone walls.

This last stone fort was part of the new Roman series of Saxon Shore forts on both sides of the English Channel. The new rectangular fort was manned by soldiers of the Second Legion and defended by high walls of flint and stone with regular towers on all sides.

There was a single gate in the centre of each side, with a double row of external ditches, save on the west, where the Roman builders dug three ditches, apparently by mistake. Most of the buildings within these strong walls were of timber, except for the bathouse on the mansio site, and a pair of stone buildings that might be temples.

Roman rule came to an end in the early 5th century when the last troops were withdrawn, but Richborough continued to be occupied, as evidenced by a small Saxon chapel near the earlier mansio. The chapel, dedicated to St Augustine, was built in the late Saxon period (c. 900) with a rectangular nave and chancel and a west porch. in the 12th century, a rounded apse was added at the eastern end, and the chapel was finally pulled down in the 17th century.

The Roman Amphitheatre

Though English Heritage promotes the nearby amphitheatre as part of the Richborough experience, it is not signposted, nor is access terribly straightforward. We had to ask the attendant at the visitor centre, and she showed us an aerial photograph and explained how to reach the site by footpath.

Even then, we mistook the way and wandered about until we chanced upon the right location. And having taken the trouble to reach the site, we found the amphitheatre to be a disappointment. Though it certainly looked impressive in the aerial view, at ground level there is little to see beyond a depression in the broad hilltop. If you are interested in seeing the amphitheatre I suggest a good OS map, or at the very least get good directions from the visitor centre!

Lest that sound too negative, let me counter that by repeating just how impressive we found Richborough fort. The scale of the earthworks and the height of the walls was enormously impressive. It truly is a remarkable site, full of interest. I loved it!

Roman Painted House

The remains of Roman 'mansio', or Official Hotel, dating to at least the 3rd century AD. The remains are surrounded by a purpose-built museum, and show extensive wall paintings and mosaics, a hypocaust (underfloor heating system), and remains of defensive fortifications.

An unusual survivor
Many Roman buildings in Britain had painted walls but very little has survived the ravages of time. It is quite astonishing that so much of the painted walls here have survived, but it took a quite unique set of circumstances to preserve them. Over 400 square feet of wall-plaster survives in its original location, by far the largest area in Britain and arguably the best Roman paintings north of the Alps. So how did the Dover painted walls survive when so little is preserved elsewhere?

The answer lies with the Roman army. In 270AD the army requisitioned the house as part of a new fort wall. They demolished part of the building and built a wall through the middle. Most of Room 3 and all of Room 2 were behind the new wall. The walls were left standing to a height of 6 feet (interior) and up to 9 feet (exterior), while the entire site was backfilled with rubble, plaster, soil and clay as part of the bank supporting the new fort wall. So the painted chambers were effectively sealed, preventing decay from weathering.

When the painted house interior was uncovered by archaeologists, the walls were still much as they had been in 270AD, showing the original Roman designs and colourful pattern of decoration. The painted house is housed in a modern building - or perhaps I should say it is housed 'under' a modern building, for when you enter the museum you find yourself on a walkway looking down into the house and fort walls. Each section of the hose is clearly labelled, and there are information panels around the walls of the walkway to explain the history of the building and exactly what each room was used for. One of the interesting features - apart from the paintings themselves - are the later medieval additions discovered by archaeologists, including medieval pits dug through the floors of the Roman rooms. Thankfully these pits did not impact the paintings on the walls.

After viewing the Painted House from above, you can descend via stairs to the house level and get a closer look at the exterior of the house, the exposed room walls, and the later fort walls and bastion tower foundations. There are several exposed sections of flue, directing heat from the hypocaust system through the walls. So the residents of the Painted House not only had underfloor heating but heated walls as well.

I thought that some of the displays could use a bit of updating, but there is a LOT of interesting information on the house and the span of Roman history in and around Dover.

Historic towns and villages in Kent

Appledore, Kent

A village on the edge of Romney Marsh, Appledore overlooks the historic Royal Military Canal, built in 1804 as a measure against French invasion. The village used to be on the banks of the Rother, but the river changed course. An earlier waterway is the 13th-century Rhee Wall, built to carry away silt from the marshes.

The origins of the village name are uncertain, but it may come from the Saxon word for an apple tree. The Danes certainly knew

Appledore, for they landed here in AD 892 to launch an invasion of England. The French did the same in 1380 when they burned the village and destroyed the church.

In the following year, the men of Appledore joined the Peasant's Revolt, and broke into Horne's Place manor house, stealing 10 pounds worth of goods. Appledore also joined Jack Cade's Revolt in 1450.

St Peter And St Paul Church

Appledore's church dates to the 13th century. The oldest parts of the building are the north chapel and west tower, the only parts of the building to escape damage during the French raid of 1380.

The remainder of the church was so badly damaged by the French that it had to be rebuilt. Some roof timbers survive, and there is a very fine 15th-century screen and medieval floor tiles. You can still see fire marks on the tower arch.

The font is later than the rebuilding; probably 15th century. In front of the altar is buried Sir Philip Chute, standard-bearer to Henry VIII. In the churchyard are 18th-century gravestones and chest tombs.

Horne's Place Chapel

Attached to the manor of Horne's Place, outside the main village, is a late 14th-century chapel, now in the care of English Heritage. The chapel stands on a vaulted cellar, with a well set into the cellar floor. The best feature is the ornate east window, but there is also a timber roof built around 1520. It is rare to find a private chapel from the medieval period, so Horne's Place is unusual, if not totally unique.

There are very enjoyable footpaths along the Royal Military Canal, where you can see pillboxes built during the World Wars. If you fancy some refreshment after walking along the canal there are 3 pubs in the village; the Crown, the Black Lion, and the Ferry Inn.

Ashford, Kent

A market town in central Kent, Ashford was likely settled in the late 9th century and was incorporated as a town in 1423. Ashford was the home of Jack Cade, leader of the uprising known as Cade's Rebellion. The parish church is largely 13th century, with 15th-century additions.

History
The town's name tells a lot about its origins; the name Ashford means a grove of ash trees near a ford. It this case the ford was

across the River Stour, and the ford was the reason why a settlement grew up. The area was settled as long ago as the Iron age, as evidenced by a barrow mound on Barrow Hill.

The Romans found iron ore in the Ashford area and established a number of mines in the region. Ashford served as a central point for the Weald, and iron ore was brought here to be processed.

The Roman town stood north of the present town centre, which grew up after a Danish raid in AD 893 caused local residents to gather together. A Saxon lord granted the residents a plot of land to build a fortified town to resist further Danish attacks. At the time of the Domesday Book, Ashford manor was owned by Hugh de Montford, the powerful Constable of England.

A Local Mystery
Richard Plantagenet (1469 - 1550) was a bricklayer working at Eastwell, just outside Ashford. Richard claimed to be the son of Richard III, which would have made him rightful king of England, though he apparently made no claim to the throne. Plantagenet is buried at Eastwell, and his grave can be visited. A modern theory suggests that he may have been Richard, Duke of York, one of the Princes in the Tower.

Ashford owes much of its post-medieval prosperity to its location. Just as the original settlement grew up around a ford, so in the 19th century Ashford found itself at a meeting of major rail lines, and its role as a train hub guaranteed continuous growth into the 20th century.

Unfortunately, much of that growth swept away the historic buildings in Ashford's town centre, save for a cluster of timber-framed buildings on Middle Row, near the church. St Mary's is the oldest building in Ashford. It dates to the 13th century and boasts a notable memorial brass to the first rector.

The church was enlarged in the 15th century by John Fogge, who is buried in the church. In the 17th century, a grammar school was founded within the churchyard. The school building now serves as a local museum.

Three miles away is Godinton Manor, a brick manor on the site of a 12th-century hall. The manor is set in beautiful gardens which are open to the public.

About Ashford
Address: *Ashford, Kent, England*
Attraction Type: Town

Aylesford, Kent

Aylesford is a large village on the River Medway, accessed via a medieval five-arched bridge. There has been human settlement here since Neolithic times, as evidenced by the long barrows of Kits Coty to the north of the village.

Today Aylesford retains its historic core, but the settlement has spread along the river in both directions, with railroad works and a busy shopping outlet bringing a modern bustle further from the historic centre.

History

Aylesford seems to have attracted famous battles throughout British history; Hengest the Jute fought the British leader Vortigern here in 455 AD, King Alfred defeated the Danes in 893 AD, and Edmund Ironside did likewise in 1016, pursuing the fleeing invaders all the way from Otford and killing many by the time they reached Aylesford. And the royals kept coming; William the Conqueror took Aylesford manor for himself after the Norman Conquest.

The origins of the village are a matter of some mystery. Legend has it that a local; chieftain named Aegel controlled a river crossing, and thus the village was known as Aegel's ford, which in time became shortened to Aylesford. The river provided a boost to commerce during the Middle Ages and into the 18th century with barges carrying goods up and down the waterway.

The parish church of St Peter and St Paul dates to the Norman period, and probably existed long before then. It may have served travellers crossing the ford, who could pause and pray for a safe crossing or give thanks for successfully completing the passage. The double-nave and chancel are out of alignment, possibly because they were built at different periods.

The oldest part of the building is the base of the tower. Within the church are the 17th-century Colepepper tomb, a memorial brass set in the chapel floor, and several funerary helmets and swords hanging in the chapel and chancel.

The most iconic structure in Aylesford is not the church, however, but the 14th-century bridge that still carries traffic over the River Medway into the village.

Of the historic buildings remaining in Aylesford among the most striking is the mid-Victorian mansion of Preston Hall. Architectural historian Nikolaus Pevsner was not impressed with Preston Hall, calling it 'hard to love'.

The Hall was built in 1849 for Edward Betts by architect John Thomas. The result is either a lovely example of Victorian Gothic or a ponderous attempt at gentility by an architect who wasn't up to the task, depending on your taste. The Hall has long since passed from private ownership and now serves as a nursing home.

Near the village is Aylesford Priory, a restored medieval monastic house of Carmelite friars that dates to 1242. After the Reformation, the friary was sold into private hands, and the monastic buildings were converted into a luxurious mansion. In 1949 the Carmelite order bought the site and re-founded it, restoring many original medieval features. The historic highlight is the Pilgrim's Hall, built around 1280.

Barfreston, Kent

The village of Barfreston was a stopover place during the Middle Ages for pilgrims visiting the shrine of St Thomas a Becket in Canterbury. Today, this once important place is little more than a peaceful hamlet set in quite attractive wooded lanes and fields.

There is a very nice village pub, but the primary reason to visit Barfreston is to see the church of St Nicholas, a 12th-century gem that is a wonderful example of Norman architecture. The church has richly carved mouldings and doorways. Above the south door is a carving thought to be the first representation of Thomas a Becket following his death.

A unique feature of Barfreston church is that the church bell is hung, not from a bellcote, but from the branches of a yew tree just outside the church.

Immediately behind the church is Barfreston Manor, an early 18th-century manor house listed Grade II to heritage interest. The manor is built of red brick and stands 2 storeys high, over a basement level.

The manor of Barfreston belonged to the Archbishop of Canterbury prior to the Norman Conquest. After the Conquest it was granted to Odo, Bishop of Bayeux, then to the Norman lord Hugh de Port, the new Constable of Dover.

Barfreston lies on the Miner's Way Trail, a long-distance footpath linking Kent locations with a history of coal mining.

Benenden, Kent

A lovely Wealden village near Tenterden, with a long, broad village green where cricket is played in the summer. There are two excellent pubs, the Bull Inn and the Duke of Wellington, located near the large village green, which is lined with attractive half-timbered houses. At the top of the green is the parish church of St George.

On the outskirts of Benenden lies Benenden girls school, begun in 1924, using the buildings of Hemsted House, a historic house built by the first Lord Cranbrook in 1857, on the foundations of a much, much older house.

Following the Norman Conquest, the manor of Benenden was given by William the Conqueror to his half-brother Odo, Bishop of Bayeux. The village was mentioned in the Domesday Book of 1086, by which time it had already acquired a parish church, one of only four villages in the Weald important enough to do so.

The manor was granted to the Guldeford family by Richard II, and later visited by Elizabeth I. Hemsted House was sold in 1716 to Sir John Norris, Admiral of the Fleet. North's grandson, also named John, married an infamous courtesan named Kitty Fisher in 1766. Fisher, whose real name was Catherine Marie Fischer, is remembered in the children's rhyme:

Lucy Locket lost her pocket
Kitty Fisher found it

Fisher was extremely popular among the villagers of Benenden, and had a reputation for generosity to the poor; unfortunately, she died only four months after her marriage, either from smallpox or, perhaps, from the effects of using lead-based cosmetics. She was buried in the Norris family vault in Benenden church. The graves of later Lords Cranbrook can be seen in the churchyard.

Two Roman roads lead through the parish, and there is evidence of Iron Age settlements. There are over 20 Wealden hall houses in the village dating from 1470-1500, suggesting that Benenden was a very prosperous place in the Middle Ages. Much of this prosperity was based upon cloth making, and many people were involved in the creation of cloth, from weaving, dyeing, fulling, and sheering.

St George's church originally had a large detached steeple, but this was struck by lightning in 1672.

There are several historic almshouses in the village, including an 18th-century house in The Street. Nearby is Queen's Well, built to commemorate the Golden Jubilee of Queen Victoria in 1887. Across from the well is St George's Club, built in 1881 by George Devey for Lord Cranbrook.

There are several interesting historic buildings fronting onto the Green, including 17th-century Clevelands, the Edmond Gibbon School (1609). At one corner is the Bull Inn, a picturesque pub dating to circa 1608.

The village sign at the bottom of the green says a lot about this lovely village; it shows a man in a top hat playing cricket on the green. Sure enough, when we visited, modern cricketers were enjoying themselves on the wicket in the centre of the green, just behind the village sign!

The church of St George stands at the top of the green. It is a largely 14th and 15th-century building, restored in the 18th and again in the 19th century. Within the church are memorials to the Norris and Gathorne-Hardy families.

Benenden is an absolute delight; a lovely, peaceful Wealden village full of historic interest.

Biddenden, Kent

The 12th century Siamese twins called the Biddenden Maids are still remembered in the town sign, and the dole they established is still distributed annually

A village famous as the birthplace of the Biddenden Maids, a pair of Siamese twins who were joined at the hip and shoulder. Marie and Eliza Chulkhurst were born in Biddenden in 1100 and lived here to a respectable age (for that era) of 34. When they died they left 18 acres of land, the income from which was to provide an annual dole of bread and wine to the poor of the parish.

This 'Biddenden Dole' is distributed each year on Easter Monday, along with biscuits imprinted with a likeness of the Maids, to anyone who requests it. The Biddenden Maids were quite famous during their lifetimes, and are remembered in the village sign on the small, triangular green.

The village High Street is lined with some extremely attractive half-timbered medieval and Jacobean buildings, aligned on either side of a cobbled pavement. Many of these are old weavers cottages, as weaving was the core economic activity of this area of the Weald for many years. This clothing heritage is remembered in the impressive Cloth Hall, just north of the green.

The church of All Saints at Biddenden is mainly 13th and 14th century, with a collection of interesting memorial brasses.

Broadstairs, Kent

A seaside town on the Isle of Thanet, in northeastern Kent, Broadstairs was settled as early as the Roman occupation. The village was initially a fishing port, but later became prosperous a centre of shipbuilding.

As early as the Saxon period a shrine stood atop the cliffs overlooking the wide bay. The site was known as Bradstow, meaning a wide place. In the 14th century, a small fishing community grew up at the base of the cliffs. It was called Broadstairs after a set of steps leading up the cliffs to the shrine. From this small fishing village, the modern town of Broadstairs developed.

The Saxon shrine lives on the shape of St Mary's Chapel, built in 1601 on the site of the Shrine of Our Lady, Bradstowe (otherwise known as the Shrine of Our Lady Star of the Sea). The shrine was a major destination for medieval pilgrims.

When sailing past the shrine, ships would dip their topsails as a mark of respect. The shrine and chapel are the oldest buildings in Broadstairs and stand near the harbour on Albion Street, at its junction with Alexandra Road.

The 16th century York Gate was part of defences erected to protect the shipyards at Broadstairs. You can still see the wishing well on Harbour Street that was used by 18th-century smugglers to hide their illegal goods from customs officers.

The Dickens Connection

The town has strong connections with author Charles Dickens, who was a regular visitor, and there is an annual Dickens festival.

On Victoria Parade is the Dickens House Museum. Despite the name, the author did not reside here during his time in Broadstairs; it was the residence of Miss Mary Pearson Strong, used by Dickens as the model for Miss Betsey Trotwood in his novel David Copperfield. The museum traces the life and career of the writer and his strong links to Broadstairs.

Bleak House

Rising above the harbour is the bulk of Bleak House, renamed because its owner believed it to be the one used by Dickens in his tale of the same name. Whether or not it truly is the house that inspired Dickens is a matter for debate, but the owner believed it was so, so he renamed the house! It now operates as a guest house, with the added attraction of a smuggling museum and 'Dickens' Study'.

Crampton Tower Museum

Located in a flint tower beside Broadstairs rail station, this small museum looks at the life and career of Thomas Crampton, a designer of railroads, locomotives, water works, and underground telegraph cables. It was Crampton who designed the first underwater telegraph cable across the English Channel. The tower itself served as part of the town's first water supply. One of the prize displays is an original 1860s Broadstairs stage coach.

Canterbury, Kent

One of the most historic of English cities, Canterbury is famous for its medieval cathedral. There was a settlement here before the Roman invasion, but it was the arrival of St Augustine in 597 AD that was the signal for Canterbury's growth. Augustine built a cathedral within the city walls and a new monastery outside the walls. The ruins of St Augustine's Abbey can still be seen today.

Initially, the abbey was more important than the cathedral, but the murder of St Thomas a Becket in 1170 changed all that. Pilgrims flocked to Canterbury to visit the shrine of the murdered archbishop, and Canterbury Cathedral became the richest in the land. It was expanded and rebuilt to become one of the finest examples of medieval architecture in Britain.

But there is more to Canterbury than the cathedral. The 12th century Eastbridge Hospital was a guesthouse for pilgrims and features medieval wall paintings and a Pilgrim's Chapel. The old West Gate of the city walls still survives, and the keep of an 11th-century castle.

St Dunstan's church holds a rather gruesome relic; the head of Sir Thomas More, executed by Henry VIII. The area around the cathedral is a maze of twisting medieval streets and alleys, full of historic buildings. Taken as a whole, Canterbury is one of the most satisfying historic cities to visit in England.

Charing, Kent

Charing is a small village of attractive cottages and the remains of an 11th-century palace used by the Archbishops of Canterbury. Charing was a stopover place on the major pilgrim trail to the shrine of Thomas a Becket at Canterbury.

The village has a wealth of historic buildings, and these are outlined in a Village Trail leaflet put out by the Charing and District Local History Society, and available at a number of local outlets. In addition, there is a village tourist map detailing many of these historic buildings.

Chief among these is the Bishop's Palace, used by the Archbishops of Canterbury as a stopping place between their residences in London and Canterbury. The palace is located behind a high wall just before the church. It was reportedly a favourite residence of Thomas Becket. He would not have recognised the present buildings, though; these date from the early 14th century.

The very large great hall of the palace is now a barn, the top of which can be seen from the churchyard. The private apartments of the archbishop face the main gates which give onto the former market place. In an interesting historical touch, the Archbishop of Canterbury still robes in the Palace when he visits Charing.

The parish church of St Peter and St Paul dates from the 13th century (chancel and nave), with the addition of transepts in the 14th century. The striking tower was added in the 15th century.

Tucked behind the church on Vicarage Close are two historic buildings, the oldest dating to the 14th century and thought to be the oldest building in Charing. The second building, the current vicarage, dates to the 15th century and was originally the church hall before being converted into a dwelling.

Closer to the High Street at Number 4, The Market Place is a half-timbered dwelling that was formerly the poor house. On the rear wall is a small window through which alms were given to poor travellers.

Along the High Street are a number of fascinating historic buildings. The most interesting may be Peirce House (yes, that's the correct spelling). This is a lovely half-timbered house set back from the road behind a high wall. Over the door are the arms of the Brents and Nevilles, celebrating the 1501 marriage of Margaret Brent to George Neville, Lord Abergavenny.

Another interesting building is Elizabethan Court, built in the 16th century. Originally timber, it was refaced in brick in the 17th century. It was once a coaching inn called The Swan, and it still boasts the cast iron brackets that carried the inn sign.

More modern is Venture Works, 20th-century home of the Cackett family, who invented the early motorcycle called the Invicta. A very early petrol pump still stands outside the house. Across the A20 from the upper High Street is The Old House, a charmingly askew half-timbered building dating to the Jacobean period. This was once a poor house.

The village of Charing was granted to the Church of Canterbury in AD 765-80 by Egbert II, King of Kent. The manor remained in the hands of the Archbishop of Canterbury until the Reformation.

Chatham, Kent

A historic port town on the Medway River in eastern Kent, Chatham grew up around a naval dockyard. The dockyard was established by Elizabeth I in 1568 and closed in 1984. It is today one of the most popular visitor attractions in south-east England.

Over the years a number of forts were built to protect the docks, including Upnor Castle (across the river), Fort Amherst, and Fort Pitt. Charles Dickens lived in Chatham as a child and featured it in several of his books.

Royal Dockyards

Easily the most popular historic attraction in the Chatham area, the Dockyards are built around a remarkable collection of historic buildings dating to the 17th century. See a Victorian rope works still used for manufacturing naval rope. Board a historic submarine, 19th-century sailing ship, and see the huge sheds where boats were made and repaired for centuries.

Chatham's Old Town Hall houses the Brook Theatre, an arts centre for dance, theatre, music, exhibitions, and art workshops. The Hall was built in 1899 to a design by GE Bond in a Renaissance style.

The town dates back to at least the 9th century, and it was mentioned in the Domesday Book of 1086. The location suggests a much older origin, however, for Chatham stands on an ancient Celtic trackway later paved and reused by the Romans to create Watling Street.

There was little more than a small village here until the 16th century when warships began to take advantage of the sheltered moorings off Gillingham. Elizabeth I decided to create a dockyard to service the fleet, and the Royal Nava;l Dockyards at Chatham were born.

The dockyards were initially only used for refitting vessels but later expanded to become a centre for shipbuilding. The dockyards needed to be defended, and Fort Amhurst was begun in 1756. Late fortifications were added to protect from attack by land. Fort Pitt was added in 1806, and a third ring of forts from 1859.

All the extra military presence at Chatham led to a huge increase in the population. The centre of Chatham is now filled with Victorian houses and public buildings, the result of the naval presence in Chatham that really only died down when the dockyards closed.

Local landmarks - aside from the Royal Naval dockyards - include the Naval Memorial on Great Lines, between Chatham and neighbouring Gillingham.

The Dickens Connection
Author Charles Dickens grew up in Chatham, and in later years he described that period as the happiest period of his childhood. He returned to Chatham much later in life and purchased a house at Gad's Hill. He incorporated many local scenes in his novels.

Maidstone, Kent
A popular town on the River Medway in north-east Kent, Maidstone is an administrative centre and the foremost market town in the county. The remains of a 14th-century archbishop's palace built by the Archbishops of Canterbury stand beside the parish church. The remains of the palace banqueting hall still stand.

The old palace stables now house the Tyrwhitt-Drake Museum of Carriages. Maidstone Museum displays finds of local archaeology - and there are a lot, for the area was heavily settled by the Romans. There are also iguanodon bones, for that dinosaur was first discovered near Maidstone in the Victorian period.

On Earl Street is the home of Andrew Broughton, former Mayor of Maidstone and Clerk to the High Court of Justice in London. It was Broughton who read out the death sentence of Charles I.

We have mentioned the parish church of St Nicholas. This is a late 14th-century building erected by Archbishop Courtenay. It has been called the finest Perpendicular church in England - a bold claim, but perhaps justified. The heavy buttresses supporting the tower give it the air of a castle.

And speaking of castles, one of the most romantic English castles stands at Leeds, just 5 miles away. This is a lovely 12th-century former royal fortress on an island in a lake.

Folkestone, Kent

Folkestone is a resort town in south-east Kent, known today for the Channel Tunnel, but formerly a popular seaside destination for holidaymakers. The older part of town is a lovely mix of

Georgian buildings, cobbled streets, and a long, sweeping promenade along the seafront.

A famous native of Folkestone was William Harvey, the medical pioneer who first described the circulation of the blood. Harvey's father was a jurat and later mayor of Folkestone, and young William was educated here before going on to Kings School in Canterbury and then to Cambridge University. Harvey's mother is buried in the parish church of Saint Mary and St Eanswythe, which dates to at least the 13th century.

The church is named for Eanswythe, the 7th-century daughter of King Eadbald of Kent. Eanswythe refused to marry, and in AD 630 she founded a nunnery at Folkestone, near the site of her father's royal castle. The nunnery stood somewhere in The Bayle area, near the current church dedicated to St Mary and Eanswythe herself.

Eanswythe was made a saint soon after her death in AD 640 - family connections certainly helped speed up the process of canonisation! In the 12th century, her relics were reburied in the chancel of the medieval church, and the site of her grave became a destination for pilgrims. So popular did Eanswythe become that she was made the town's patron saint.

A Saintly Mystery

The saint's relics were hidden at the Dissolution of the monasteries to protect them from Henry VIII's commissioners. Then in 1885 workmen undertaking repairs to the area of the high altar unearthed a lead casket hidden in the north wall. The casket most certainly dates to the Saxon period and held bone fragments of a woman in her 30s.

Were these the bones of Folkestone's saint? The casket was put on display in the chancel, and are revered today as those of Eanswythe, though of course, we cannot be certain that they are actually Eanswythe's remains.

In the 13th century, Folkestone joined other major port towns along the south coast as part of the Cinque Ports, and the status led the town to a period of great prosperity and trading wealth. Despite this ancient status, Folkestone remained a small town, with an economy based mostly on fishing.

Even the development of Folkestone harbour by the famous engineer Thomas Telford in 1809 did not bring any great growth. It was the coming of the railway that turned Folkestone into a busy destination for holidaymakers.

Much of the town's architecture comes from the Victorian era, when the town developed as a popular resort, with seaside entertainment and promenades. One public space surviving from this period is the Kingsnorth Garden and there is a Victorian bandstand at Leas Cliff.

On a cliff over Copt Point stands a Martello Tower, built in 1809 as part of a string of coastal defences to deter a French invasion. Just outside the town are two military memorials; the Kent Battle of Britain Memorial and the Battle of Britain Memorial at Capel-le-Ferme

The End

Printed in Great Britain
by Amazon

85627722R00138